From Sirius
to Earth

A Therapist Discovers
A Soul Exchange

Evelyn Michelle Fuqua, Ph.D.
and
Athor

Published by
Inner Eye Books
an imprint of
OUGHTEN HOUSE PUBLICATIONS
LIVERMORE, CA USA

From Sirius To Earth
by Evelyn Fuqua, Ph.D. and Athor

Published by
Inner Eye Books
an imprint of
OUGHTEN HOUSE PUBLICATIONS
PO Box 2008
LIVERMORE, CALIFORNIA 94551 USA
PHONE: (510) 447-2332
FAX: (510) 447-2376
E-MAIL: oughten@oughtenhouse.com
INTERNET: www.oughtenhouse.com

Library of Congress Cataloging in Publication
Fuqua, Evelyn Michelle.
    From Sirius to earth : a journey remembered : a therapist discovers soul exchange / Evelyn Michelle Fuqua and Athor.
            p. cm.
    ISBN 1-880666-65-0
    1. Fuqua, Evelyn Michelle. 2. Sirius--Miscellaneous. 3. Spirit writings.
    4. Reincarnation. I. Athor. II. Title.
    BF1301.F96 1997
    133.9'3--dc21
                                                    97-20521
                                                    CIP

ISBN 1-880666-65-0

                PRINTED IN THE USA

Table Of Contents

Dedication

**Dedicated to all the Beings of Light in Earth
bodies working toward the evolution of
planet Earth**

"Many beings do not realize what a grand and glorious place this Planet Earth can be. They do not realize that it is not simply a school for those who have not yet learned, but rather a most marvelous testing ground for the souls and beings of every level and plane, verily unto the Godhead itself.

"Do not look upon yourselves as limited creatures, as limited beings, for you are all the same. You are all dancing lights in the infinite firmament of God. Each of you twinkles and radiates as the stars in the heaven do.

"Those of you who suffer here and wish perhaps that you were else-where, look out upon the night sky. Look out upon the twinkling stars up in the Father's heaven and know that is indeed what you all are. You are there as well as here. And indeed you are everywhere."

— *Athor, channeling Christ Consciousness*

Acknowledgments

Evelyn

I would like to thank the following people who helped in birthing the Athor book project:

Wally, my husband, who understood very little of my work with Athor but still supported me in the project because he believed in me. Wally had acute leukemia and graduated to the Higher Realms in October, 1994.

Sylvia Havens, our typist, for her tremendous patience in making numerous changes in the text over the two years we continued to add information in order to clarify the Athor story.

Timothy Gilbert, who programmed the original disks into my new computer, did the final editing on the text, and put it into a format suitable to send to a publisher. His support in this project helped greatly in making it a reality.

Kay Baugh and Juanita Montague, faithful friends, who made suggestions and selected words for the glossary.

Athor and the Council of Twelve on Sirius, who had their own timetable for disclosing the history of Rose-Athor. Athor was insistent on getting all the pieces of the puzzle. This was a great lesson in patience for me. I honor Athor for her willingness to bare her soul in order to allow others to know her truth.

Athor

I would like to thank the following individuals who helped shape the raw ethereal essence into tangible form:

Evelyn, for her great patience in working with my other-worldly time frames, for her dogged persistence in the face of many obstacles and frustrations, for her much valued friendship, her love of truth, foresight, and courage to continue in this endeavor to educate others.

Christopher, for his emotional support of my endeavors.

All of my friends (who are too numerous to mention individually but who know who they are) who stood by me in this undertaking.

Last, but not least, I wish to thank my Council and Spiritual Beings of Light who have made all of this possible, and all humankind to whom it is given and without whom there would have been no need.

Thank you all!

Namaste

Preface

Once in a great while a therapist has a client who makes such an impact that she is compelled to re-examine her belief system. Such was the case with Rose-Athor.

I had attended the International Association of Metaphysicians' conference held at the University of Denver in 1986. One of the main speakers was Carol Parrish-Harra, who told her story of feeling that she was definitely a different person after a near-death experience. She was an articulate speaker who conveyed total sincerity and thus convinced me that perhaps this Walk-In phenomenon was really a possibility.

While at the conference, I met another so-called Walk-In, Ruth Soderstrom, who along with Carol, was featured in Ruth Montgomery's book, *Threshold to Tomorrow*. Montgomery's book describes a number of people who were identified by her "Guides" as Walk-Ins. Ruth was in my public speaking group during the conference. We each practiced speaking in front of a video camera, viewing ourselves as we spoke. When it was Ruth's turn, she talked about how she had been so painfully introverted that she was reluctant to reply to strangers who attempted to talk to her on a bus. Her personality changed dramatically after a bout of severe depression in which she, like Carol, became aware of a profound transformation in her life. It was after her Walk-In experience that she began giving lectures and writing books.

I left the conference believing there was at least a possibility of the occurrence of a Walk-In experience in which one soul leaves and a more highly evolved soul takes its place in the body. Even then, however, I was somewhat skeptical because I had never had any firsthand experience with this kind of phenomenon.

Then I met Rose-Athor, a client who came to me in late 1988. It was apparent early in the therapy that Rose was probably a Soul Exchange Entity (SEE), a term we feel is much more definitive than Walk-In. The term was coined by another of my clients, Kathryn-Zonatar, who came to me later in 1990 for therapy as a result of her own dramatic transformation in personality. I later learned that Carol Parrish-Harra also refers to herself as a Soul Exchange.

"Athor" is the name of the new soul that entered Rose's body when she was a child of three years and two months. Athor's case required almost three years of therapy before we finally unraveled the bizarre history of why Athor volunteered to enter the body of Rose, who has Environmental Illness and came from a background of mentally abusive parents.

At the beginning of therapy, it was extremely difficult for either Rose or me to believe that she was actually a Soul Exchange. I had never heard of this kind of experience taking place when one was a child. Also, in the cases cited by Ruth Montgomery, my impression had been that the old soul was always replaced by a soul who had evolved to a higher level through many incarnations on Earth.

In Athor's case, not only had the entering soul seemingly never incarnated on Earth before, but the data coming through the regressions indicated that Athor was an aspect of a Being of Light, a member of the Council of Twelve on the star system Sirius.

I am not exactly a typical therapist. I specialized mainly in past-life regression therapy after my retirement from the school system in 1987 so this was a totally new experience as a therapist. I had no one to turn to for advice since, to my knowledge, there were no written references about such cases in psychological literature, or even any therapists dealing with the Soul Exchange phenomenon.

The vast majority of therapists probably had significant doubts that it was even possible for one soul to exchange places with another. As a consequence, all of the therapy with Rose-Athor was conducted strictly through the use of my intuitive sense of what seemed to be appropriate at the time. I made it clear to Rose (the name of the person she thought she was) that, since I was not charging for the therapy, this would be considered research.

I indicated from the beginning that I had strong reservations about working with a client whose background indicated a possibility of psychosis. I did not believe this was true in her case, but for the first few months of therapy, I kept wondering if this were a case of possession or multiple-personality. Therefore, I was not really sure of my diagnosis for some time. When the mental health community begins to accept the possibility of transformational occurrences which change one's reality, a new section will need to be added to the Diagnostic and Statistical Manual of Mental Disorders (DMS-III). It certainly does not list Soul Exchange Trauma.

Despite my hesitancy to accept her case, Rose was quite anxious for me to work with her. She was in a constantly life-threatening situation with her Environmental Illness, an illness where patients are allergic to so many substances that they often need to live in a totally controlled environment. This is almost impossible to do if one attempts to lead any kind of normal life, and Rose insisted on forcing herself to go out into the world as much as she could manage. However, she suffered the consequence of almost daily allergic attacks which were often severe enough to make her feel that she was close to death. Rose has never been willing to live in total isolation like many of those with this illness do.

For many years she had sought the help of various physicians and therapists in an attempt to improve her situation. Rose had always been a strong believer in the power of the mind over the body. Therapists with strong metaphysical beliefs, like my own, still seem to be quite difficult to find. Therefore, she seemed to feel from the beginning that I could help her, despite my feelings to the contrary.

From the first session, I realized that this was like no other case I had encountered. I made the decision early in therapy to use Rose as my cotherapist, requesting feedback from her at each session to help explain the information that emerged from her regression. While this was not a conscious decision, it was very clear to me that Athor would tell me what to do, and I would follow her instructions. I realized that this was unconventional and not very professional, but I also sensed it was the only approach that would work for her.

Rose is naturally quite analytical, a trait that does not seem to go with psychic abilities, but we later learned that the beings on Sirius specialize in technology. Rose-Athor is also exceptionally intelligent. If she had the credentials, she would make an excellent psychologist.

Fortunately, both Rose-Athor and I have a good sense of humor. We would often end a session by laughing a great deal to break the tension of an intense therapy session in which almost unbelievable facts emerged. I also had a difficult time knowing which name to use in addressing her and I felt like an idiot when trying to use her name during the hypnosis sessions. I often used the names of Rose and Athor interchangeably because once we had established that the soul of Rose was no longer in her body, I knew she was really Athor. That was the name I had the most difficulty using.

Extraterrestrial names (I've encountered several over the past three years) do not seem natural for Earthlings to use. Fortunately, this has never bothered Athor but early in therapy, I would laughingly ask, "Who are you, anyway?" when I found myself using the old name. Fortunately, we both perceived the humor in the situation.

This book is the result of four months of intensive therapy, followed by periodic therapy as the need arose, for almost three years from the time Rose first came to me in December, 1988. The first six months involved much repetition of the Soul Exchange experience in order to discharge the tremendous emotion connected to the event, and to extract as many details as possible. During succeeding hypnosis sessions, we established the past life connections of both the Rose soul and the Athor soul, which afforded the preparation for the exchange. We discovered that such an exchange can take place only if there is a prior agreement between the two souls.

Parts of the puzzle came through slowly, until Athor was able to relive the story of all the various traumatic experiences the body had experienced in this lifetime—and prior lifetimes—as well as the trauma which the Athor soul had suffered when it once tried and failed to be a Soul Exchange during the time of Jesus. We found that the Rose soul was a very highly evolved soul who had earned the right to end its cycles of incarnations on Earth.

Increasingly, Athor felt that she was Athor and not Rose. In fact, it became increasingly difficult to regress Athor back into the Rose lifetime because she felt it was a waste of time. She would repeatedly state under hypnosis that we were exploring the roots of another person, and then she would sigh and proceed as instructed, apparently just to please me.

We had decided by then that a book should be written about the Rose-Athor case. I was insistent that we repeat any parts of the story that were not perfectly clear. We both concluded that the therapy was not going to cure her illness as we had hoped. Therefore, as far as I was concerned, the sessions increasingly became research and Athor rather resented this. She was often bored telling the "same old story" again but for me, if the same facts surfaced each time, it was further evidence of a genuine Soul Exchange. Repeatedly, we would get the same basic story, with additional details from each succeeding regression, making it definitely worthwhile.

After the second year of therapy, I kept insisting that we now had all the pieces of the puzzle, but Athor still thought there was more information we needed in order to answer the underlying question of why she would agree to enter such a damaged body. As it turns out, she was right. Apparently, it was a matter of timing because the remaining evidence to solve the puzzle emerged.

This happened in late December, 1991, almost exactly three years after beginning therapy. Apparently, the "plan" seems to have been that the therapy be completed before 1992 because during Athor's participation in the 11:11 Event on January 11, 1992, she became aware that this was a major shift for her.

Finally, by the end of 1991, Athor was able to break through the blocks of a very painful memory. She traced her own roots back to the Source and came forward to the time when she attempted her first devastating Soul Exchange, an experiment which did not have the approval of the Council. We now understood the guilt that motivated her to volunteer as a Soul Exchange with the Rose soul in this lifetime. It was also after her own breakthrough that Athor was able to begin tracing the souls of other people back to the Source. This has resulted in the accumulation of much fascinating data about a soul before it incarnates on Earth.

Over three years of therapy, I observed a gradual transformation in the personality of Athor. True, she still became quite ill on occasions, but my test of the effectiveness of the therapy was the change in Athor as she gradually began to truly believe she was Athor and not Rose.

Initially, I felt that Rose was a very hostile, suspicious person. This was totally understandable, considering her abusive family background and the negative experiences she encountered later in life, a result of her exceptional psychic abilities. I use the name Rose because at that time that is who she thought she was. These feelings continued for much of the first year of therapy, since this was her programming.

I once observed Rose in a group setting in a friend's home. It was a metaphysical group that I thought would be good support for Rose during the therapy process. However, she was reluctant to participate because at that point she was still somewhat confused about her identity. The group leader asked me to stop bringing Rose because she contributed nothing to the group. What a contrast her behavior is now when she attends group meetings in my home. Athor often leads the group meditation and is frequently vocal in her disagreement with some of my statements. At this point she is definitely the teacher, and I am the student.

In retrospect, this therapy seems to have been part of a master plan orchestrated by the Council of Sirius. Athor could not have come for therapy unless she suffered Environmental Illness; therefore, even that was part of the overall plan. Although the illness continued, by the second year I was hooked on solving the puzzle of Athor, therefore, I was willing to spend time on research with her, despite the lack of financial compensation. I discovered there was an agreement, on a soul level, for me to work with Athor in order to bring forth more information about the Soul Exchange phenomenon as well as with other experiments to help the Earth evolve into the fifth dimension. This understanding finally came to me in late 1991 and is discussed later in the book.

I still believe genuine S.E.E.s (Soul Exchange Entities, a term I coined) are quite rare. Since I began therapy with Athor, a number of clients have come to me believing they are Soul Exchanges. Zonatar, the client who first used the term Soul Exchange, thus replacing the Walk-In term, may also be a Soul Exchange. I saw her for only six sessions, but I can say with certainty that there was a transformation of her personality. However, it was quite different from the drastic change that took place within seconds in Athor's case.

Zonatar's initial transformation was relatively easy, but as we continued our relationship after therapy, it became evident that she needed much support in completing her transformation. Through her work with Athor and me, we learned that once an exchange occurs, the emotional, mental, and causal bodies, which make up the auric bodies of the individual, then need to be purified—burning out all the debris, so to speak—of the soul that left. This involves much emotional trauma.

According to Athor, Kathryn-Zonatar is actually an aspect of her soul that is a "future self" that made the decision to come into the body during this crucial time in order to help the Earth evolve. This concept is being explored in more depth by Shirley-Am-Ork, a highly evolved being I met at a workshop Zonatar and I presented at the Association of Past Life Research and Therapies Conference in 1991. Like Zonatar, Shirley-Am-Ork definitely thought she was a Soul Exchange. However, because Am-Ork is as interested in research as I am, she continues to try to understand exactly what happened to her. It's likely that she is an aspect of her Group Soul, another type of "future self" who agreed to come in now rather than in the future.

I have discovered that many people think they are Soul Exchanges simply because they know there was a dramatic transformation at some point in their lives and as a result, they truly do feel that they are different individuals. However, there is very often another explanation. The most common occurrence is that an aspect of the "Higher Self" comes into conscious awareness, giving people greater wisdom and access to a vast range of intuitive knowledge. This seems to be occurring to an increasing number of people.

There are other experiments, such as "Soul Braids," in which a vibrational frequency from a higher dimension joins with the original soul. Again, this is through mutual agreement on a soul level. This seems to be an experiment that is gradually being perfected, as is the "Higher Future-Self Entry." All of these transformations are very difficult for one to handle alone because there is a sudden dramatic shift in one's reality. This can cause chaos in relationships and in the workplace. One's viewpoint of life is suddenly quite different from that of the majority of people.

These new experiments do not seem quite as drastic as an actual Soul Exchange, but the individuals involved need a therapist who will give validity to the experience, rather than a diagnosis of psychosis which, unfortunately, has happened in many of these cases. Obviously, further research is needed to understand all these changes in consciousness and therapists need to be educated in order to deal with such cases.

The actual terminology for these phenomena is not particularly important. Without a consultation with Athor and her amazing psychic abilities, I would not know exactly which particular experiment was occurring with many clients of traumatic personality transformation that I have encountered. I propose that all of these be termed Walk-Ins. As to the specific experience, the experiment can vary tremendously, with some being extremely traumatic. According to Athor, each experiment is unique.

Our goal, therefore, in writing this book is threefold: (1) to assist therapists who may have clients of the Soul Exchange and/or Walk-In varieties; (2) to aid S.E.E.s in understanding themselves better, especially those who exchanged souls at a very young age and, therefore, do not have a conscious recall of the experience; and (3) to assist in raising the consciousness of humans in general by opening their minds to the possibility that such experiments are occurring.

The book is divided into two parts. Part One was written by Athor and tells her story of this lifetime, up until the time she came to me for therapy. Part Two contains discussions of the therapy. Actual transcripts are used because very few people would believe this story unless they read the transcripts of the most important therapy sessions. It is difficult reading, but readers who stick with it may find themselves transported into a different reality.

Rose is a fictitious name for the former occupant of the Athor body. Until her health improves, she prefers to keep a low profile in order to protect her Earth identity.

— *Evelyn Fuqua, 1989*

Introduction

Because the case of Athor will be difficult for most readers to believe, I feel a need to establish my credibility as a rational person. To do so I need to provide the reader with some background. There could hardly be a greater contrast between Rose-Athor's life and my own. I grew up in a secure, loving, extended-family type environment. My family was from the "Old South," with ancestors going back to the Revolutionary War.

From birth until I completed college, I lived on a large farm near the small town of Fort Valley, Georgia. I dearly loved the South and never envisioned leaving there. I would gladly have stayed in Atlanta, where I lived and taught school after graduation from college, but I married an engineer from Georgia Tech who made a career of job-hopping. He took a position in Washington, D.C., for the National Security Agency (NSA). From there we moved to Indianapolis, Indiana, where he worked for RCA.

After two years there, my husband welcomed the chance to migrate to California where, for several years, he worked at McClellan Air Force Base near Sacramento. Although the marriage resulted in a divorce after ten years of total incompatibility, I now feel that it was necessary in order for me to leave the security of the South and move to California, where I eventually would become part of a grand metaphysical movement.

During all of this moving around, I continued to teach school wherever we went. I had not intended to have a career but after trying unsuccessfully to have children for a number of years, it seemed judicious to return to college. I earned an M.A. in counseling and my relationship with my students was the part that I liked best about teaching.

I completed my M.A. and the requirements for a school counselor's credential at California State University Sacramento (CSUS) by 1964. My career as a high school counselor was going well, although my marriage slowly disintegrated. After a divorce in 1965, I took a position as a counselor for an Air Force Dependent School in Japan.

I had no strong desire to go to Japan. I had applied for Europe but, as it turned out, my year in Japan was probably highly influential in the gradual evolvement of my spiritual beliefs. There I met many wonderful people who were devout Buddhists. I wondered how these good beings could not go to Heaven.

I traveled extensively throughout the Orient, visiting numerous temples in many different countries. I continued to attend services at the base chapel but because of my contacts with Oriental cultures, I began to question the validity of many of my earlier Christian beliefs.

This questioning intensified after a trip to the South Pacific in 1968. After completing the tour, I returned to the island of Fiji, where I met an interesting man who was an East Indian Moslem. During my month's stay in Fiji, my Indian friend took me to many places where I was the only woman. I was always treated with great respect and hospitality.

With a few Christian churches on the island, the natives and Indians had the opportunity to accept Christ and Christianity. They chose, instead, to remain devoted Moslems. According to the Christian Church's tenets, they were doomed to go to Hell. This made no sense at all to me. After my positive experience in Fiji, I had to question why these beautiful people were not going to go to Heaven.

I met my late husband, Wally, in 1968, shortly after I returned from my South Pacific adventure. He was an engineering geologist for the California Department of Water Resources. Wally had worked extensively on the state water project, which principally involved construction of aqueducts, pumping plants, and tunnels—a system to deliver water to the southern end of the state.

He was transferred to Palmdale, California, in 1970, to complete the southern terminus of the project. As you can imagine, with this background he was quite left-hemisphere-dominant. His scientific mind was an interesting contrast to that of his "spacy" wife. We were married in early 1970, and I commuted to Palmdale from Sacramento periodically until the end of the school year in order to be with my husband.

During the summer I was fortunate to obtain a position in Palmdale, this time as an elementary counselor. Whereas in high school I had been dealing with scheduling and paperwork much of the time, here I did real counseling. This turned out to be quite frustrating. I often felt totally inadequate in dealing with the severe problems of these very troubled children. My supervisors thought I did a fantastic job, however. As a consequence, they added two other elementary counselors and two intermediate school counselors the following year. I interviewed for one of the intermediate positions, was selected for the job, and thus began the next phase of my school career as a counselor for seventh and eighth graders.

Then in 1975 my husband was transferred back to Sacramento. With much reluctance, I resigned my job in Palmdale to return to Northern California. We settled in Rocklin, a small community near Sacramento. Unable to find another position with the schools, I decided to return once again to California State University (CSUS) to earn a special education credential. This was the area where there were abundant job openings in schools. I finally obtained a position as an elementary counselor and resource specialist. This combination of duties was impossibly demanding and thus began an extremely frustrating period of my life.

Although I was made a full-time counselor after three years, my school continued to have massive problems. It had the highest Aid for Dependent Children (AFDC) rate of any school in the district. The population of non-English-speaking children increased yearly. The teachers were stressed out and I was as much a therapist for the teachers as for the students. I finally made the decision to take early retirement in 1987.

I had begun my practice as a licensed Marriage, Family, and Child Therapist in 1970, while still working as a counselor in the public schools in Palmdale. It was relatively easy to obtain an M.F.C.C. license at that time. It was granted on the basis of my M.A. degree, experience, and the recommendations of colleagues. Because of the demanding duties of my school job, I only had a few clients in the evenings for many years, until I finally retired.

Over the years, I became increasingly disillusioned with my effectiveness in trying to resolve the problems of troubled families and marriages. I really did not enjoy the work and even though I seemed to be fairly successful in attracting clients, it was only when I began incorporating the many metaphysical concepts I was learning into my therapy that I began to feel I was truly an effective therapist.

My conscious search for a new belief system began when my husband had been transferred to Palmdale. I first picked up a paperback entitled *The World Beyond* by Ruth Montgomery when we took a trip to Laguna Beach during Thanksgiving in 1971. This was the first book I had ever read on reincarnation. It made a great deal of sense to me, even though I had grown up in a very traditional Protestant family. My grandfather was an elder in the Presbyterian Church and two of my uncles were Presbyterian ministers. I attended Sunday school and church regularly while growing up, and daily chapel was mandatory when I attended Agnes Scott College in Decatur, Georgia. It was only through much reading and soul-searching over a period of five years that I could truly say that I believed in reincarnation.

In retrospect, I also believe some metaphysical experiences during my childhood helped me adopt this belief. My paternal grandmother used to hold seances in the old Bassett home. Although both of my father's parents were deceased by the time I was born, I grew up on tales from my father about automatic writing and table tipping so my early years were influenced by the metaphysical Bassett side of the family, as well as by the religious maternal Melton side. Interestingly, I had functioned for so long in a very left-brained linear pattern that it was only in writing this that I remembered the often-told ghost stories of my early years.

During the 1970s I still questioned everything I read in metaphysics. I needed repeated reinforcement to actually incorporate various concepts into my spiritual beliefs, but maybe my Grandmother Bassett was actually more of an influence on me than I had ever recognized before.

In 1973 I met a very wise teacher, a psychic named Maye Shaw, in Los Angeles. This was my first experience with a psychic, and even though much of what she told me made little sense at the time, I have always regarded her as a deeply spiritual, exceptionally gifted woman. One simple statement particularly impressed me: "Trust in yourself. Believe only what rings true to you." I have passed this advice on to others many times. I particularly stress this regarding the contents of this book—accept only what seems useful to you at the present time.

As part of my spiritual growth process, I became a member of A.M.O.R.C. (Rosicrucians) in 1974. It was also during the time I lived in the desert that I read about Religious Research now based in Grand Island, Florida. I obtained a Life Reading from Religious Research in 1976, with a follow-up reading in 1984. I found these readings of my soul's Earth history to be extremely helpful.

As with A.M.O.R.C., my ties with Religious Research have continued. This organization, which carries on the work of Dr. Franklin Loehr, has strongly influenced my decision to conduct research with Athor. Franklin Loehr, who channeled information from the Akashic records via his spirit guide, John Christopher Daniels, will be discussed in more detail in a forthcoming book dealing with the Athor Soul Readings.

By the time my husband was transferred back to Sacramento in 1976, I had made the decision to acquire the necessary training to use hypnosis in my private practice. At that time, anyone could do hypnosis without a license in the state of California, except for Marriage, Family, and Child Therapists (that finally changed in 1991). The training consisted of two intensive weekend seminars of basic and advanced hypnotherapy instruction, plus field work under the supervision of a psychologist.

During my supervised work in hypnosis, one of my clients was a young woman who seemed to have no explanation for her many problems in this present lifetime. When asked if she would be willing to go back to a past life to see if we could find any causes for her problems, she agreed, although she had no belief in reincarnation.

This was my first experience in past life regression work, and I was amazed when she repeatedly went back to a life in a small town in Kansas, where she was killed at the age of seventeen in an automobile accident while quite intoxicated. Her family was extremely religious and was appalled by her drinking and sexual promiscuity. She left that lifetime (1952) with tremendous feelings of guilt about sex and alcohol. Her present husband drank beer, which turned her totally off, although from what she told me his drinking did not seem excessive.

At the time of the regression, she was separated from her husband and extremely depressed. She had many sexual problems and was particularly afraid of having children (she had had one abortion without telling her husband). Repeatedly going back to that past life and to the death experience seemed to alleviate all her present-day problems. The guilt carried over from that life seemed to be the root cause of her problems. Shortly after her therapy, she returned to her husband and has since had four children.

I was so enthusiastic about this remarkable method of therapy that I decided to go back to school at the age of 48 to earn a Ph.D. in psychology. This was pretty far-out stuff, and I wanted to have as many credentials as possible in order to be credible because this was the kind of therapy I wanted to practice. A Ph.D. would not help me in the school system, but it would be an asset in private practice when I finally retired from the schools.

My goal was to write my dissertation on past-life therapy, but this never happened because the person teaching the class on dissertation writing insisted that there was no such thing as a past life and steadfastly refused to approve my proposed research. However, before my proposal was denied, my search for more information on past-life therapy led me to the Association of Past Life Research and Therapies (A.P.R.T.) in 1981. A psychologist friend who practiced past-life therapy "in the closet" was a member of A.P.R.T., and he told me about their forthcoming conference in San Francisco. I immediately signed up.

Being at the A.P.R.T. conference was a real high. Here were all these wonderful people who believed the same things I believed. I was impressed by the number of professional people attending and it gave me the confidence to continue my goal of specializing in past-life regression therapy. After the conference, I also had my first past-life regression in a group led by Helen Wambach, Ph.D., the wonderful lady who, along with Ian Stevenson, M.D. (University of Virginia), had conducted the most valid research in the study of past-life regression at that time.

Once one totally accepts that we have lived many times before, and that we are the sum total of all of our lives, one's view of reality changes. Reincarnation is the only satisfactory explanation for all the injustices on planet Earth. I found it increasingly impossible to deal with clients using traditional methods, and this was reflected in my work as a counselor in the public schools. Needless to say, although I had always received excellent evaluations from my principals, I am sure that my last principal breathed a sigh of relief when I made the decision to retire. He was aware of some of the metaphysical concepts I used with my students, but he hoped I would retire before anyone else found out he knew about it.

It becomes increasingly incomprehensible to me that any rational person fails to see the truth in reincarnation because it makes so much sense. However, once people openly declare their belief in reincarnation, it unfortunately separates them from mainstream thinking. A.P.R.T. helped me keep my sanity during the last six years of my school career when I felt very much alone in my belief system. Not only was I accepted with open arms by A.P.R.T., but I was elected to the Board of Directors for six years, serving as treasurer, then, finally, vice-president—a very demanding but rewarding position.

It was a huge relief to retire from the schools in 1987, and I began to advertise my services openly as a therapist specializing in past-life regression therapy. I continued to use many of the traditional techniques, but I increasingly integrated the metaphysical concepts I was continuing to explore.

By 1988 we had built a large addition to our home, with a lovely office adjoining an atrium, with a waterfall designed by my husband to help induce an atmosphere of total relaxation in which to conduct my hypnotherapy and regressions. I felt very comfortable with my belief system, my case load increased, and I was enjoyed doing exactly what I wanted to do professionally.

Then I met Athor. This was to begin another very disturbing period in my life. Believing in reincarnation was one thing, but having a client who was an Extraterrestrial was quite another. At times I began to doubt my own sanity. Even though it had always seemed perfectly logical to me that Extraterrestrials had visited Earth many times, and the UFO concept had always interested me, I had never had any direct experience with Extraterrestrials, UFOs, or Soul Exchanges.

I felt fascination but also tremendous confusion during the first few months of working with Athor. I began reading everything I could find about Extraterrestrials and UFOs. Although there was a fair amount of material on these subjects by 1989, I could find nothing on Soul Exchanges. Apparently, I was treading on virgin territory.

As I became increasingly convinced that what had happened to Athor was real, and that the events that subsequently happened to me were also real, I felt that this was a story that needed to be told. I did not relish the idea of writing a book myself. Writing my doctoral dissertation and a manual on the metaphysical work I had done in the schools was enough writing to last me for some time. Writing is laborious for me. I do not consider myself a particularly gifted author. I kept telling Athor that she should write a book, but she was struggling for survival with her continuing health problems, so that did not seem likely.

I agreed to describe the therapy if she would write about her life. My part of the book was almost completed before Athor finally wrote her part in 1992. I had to prod her to finish her part because her writing seemed to go at a snail's pace. But then Athor has never been very interested in Earth time.

I began to wonder if she would ever discipline herself sufficiently enough to be an author. Athor's entire section was written in longhand, much of it done while she sat in her car in secluded areas. Very little of it has been edited because editing was not necessary, which is not the case with my own writing. In my opinion, she is a gifted author, but this may be the last of her writing in print. I suspect that any published material coming from Athor in the future will be transcripts, which will come through her while in a trance state.

It's important for readers to get the flavor of Athor's thinking while she is in a fully conscious state. I appreciate her humor and her fluency with words. As you will discover, her writing has a very different vibration from that of the words channeled from her Higher Self found in the therapy section of this book.

From Sirius to Earth

Part 1 — Athor's Story

There exists upon or within Sirius something akin to the Garden of Eden. There is a Council of Elders, a group of beings who gather to determine who should be created and when. Then the determination is made as to where. There are twelve members of this council. They are Kyata, Phadrona (not exact, but closest to Earth sound), Athor, Elysia, Philomyne, Achtama, Bjirdia, Gehema, Arturius, Sarta, Eloha, and Badra.

The Council of Elders do not have physical bodies per se, but are merely a picture representation given to the mind to allow some type of visual recognition of these frequencies. The Athor-being has almost a warrior-type appearance. The visual impression brings forth a sash across the chest which is embedded with a logo similar to the lightning bolt coming through what appears to be a cloud.

I see a large being, represented as solidly physical in appearance. The eyes appear to be what you would term violet, sparkling violet eyes that give forth flashes of light. The nose is chiseled in what you term a Grecian form. The facial features are akin to those of Grecian nobility upon this plane and what is depicted as the Grecian gods.

The being wears a kind of muted gray body suit which is like a second skin. There are boot-type looking things that appear to be of some other material, and they are a silver gray color. On these so-called boots, again the emblem of the lightning appears. The hands are long, not unduly slender. The fingers are sensitive but very strong, and these are also covered in a long, glove-like thing which comes forth from the shoulder all the way to the fingers, covering all. It is almost like a uniform.

There is a collar of some sort that comes out and stands up, and the hair appears to be a very dark coloration of a most soft, extremely wavy texture, which is shoulder-length. The being is seven and one-half to eight and one-half feet tall. Athor is androgynous, although the being has a very strong masculine energy.

— Athor, November 10, 1991

Chapter I

A Psychic Childhood

U nraveling life's mysteries may often be a perilous undertaking, but it is certainly not boring. There are myriad patterns glistening in harmonious splendor in each sparkling snowflake. So, too, is the panorama of life, on this planet and elsewhere. The All That Is has generously allowed for total creativity, an infinite movement through all forms, through all ethers, and intra- and inter-galactic spaces. That creativity coursing through humankind is unbounded in its flow. It is up to each one of us to utilize it as we see fit. During my journey of wonderment, pain, pathos, and ecstasy, there has arisen in me an increasing awareness that the more I discover of life's mysteries, the more I see how much yet remains to be explored.

My earliest memories include an awareness that I did not "belong." I recall looking around when walking among others and distinctly saying to myself, "Where am I? These are not my people!" As I telepathically reached out to touch them, none seemed to respond or communicate in return. I was emotionally devastated and time froze in slow-moving increments of greater and greater bewilderment.

During the summer when I was between three and four years of age, relatives took me to a health spa. I was told to take a nap and, being accustomed to the European manner of child-rearing, I tried to comply because children did not disobey their elders. However, there was a force greater than my respect for human authority, and when it suddenly boomed, "Come out into the wheat fields, Rose," I climbed out the window and ran into the fields. This "voice" had been with me forever, and I was most accustomed to this internal communication.

Evidently, my disappearance was most prolonged. I recall the gigantic stalks of wheat far over my head, swaying in the glistening sun, turning to shadowy giants in the flickering twilight. These shadows did not frighten me because there was a figure in brilliant white Light in the fields with me. He played and communicated with me in "my" language (telepathically). I felt safe, loved, protected, and most of all, understood.

The worried vacationers finally found me, but the ecstasy I felt from meeting with this beautiful Light Being blurred all else. Soon after, my Catholic mother began teaching me about Jesus and God, and once I had heard about Jesus, a deep inner conviction arose in me. Somewhere on the planet walked a being like Christ, a being like the man of Light who had played with me. I was determined to meet that being physically.

In 1956 my stepfather decided that in order to reach America, where the streets were "paved with gold" (so the "old timers" said), we would move to Canada first. He had been offered a position with a large firm in Montreal so off we went, embarking on our journey with mixed emotions. My mother, fearing the loss of the old ways and stability, tearfully ran down the gangplank back onto shore, but my stepfather, Karl, urged her back onto the ship. The journey was one of great adventure for me. Soon I organized a "classroom" with five or ten other children aboard.

Our arrival in port was delayed ten days because of a storm on the Atlantic. The crashing walls of water tossed the ocean liner like a stick in a maelstrom and gave me my first experience of sea-sickness and a great distrust of the ocean. As of that time, I have always felt safer flying over the ocean than traveling on it. The unbounded fury of tons of water whipped by a frenzied, blowing giant over a vast expanse of unfathomable depths instills in one a sense of awe, respect, and fear. That omnipotence of an ocean in full-blown fury is a feeling—a presence—one never quite forgets.

The "great adventure" that awaited me when I first boarded the ocean liner in Europe included many twists and turns once I disembarked in Canada. One experience in particular remains etched indelibly in my memory. My parents knew a couple in rural Quebec, and one summer we all went to their farm for a vacation. My stepfather decided to take me swimming in the river, which bordered one side of the farm. I was unable to swim, and my heart was not in it, but Karl persuaded me. He told me to hold onto his back, and he would swim across with me. A little over half-way across, the current became too strong. Karl panicked and told me to let go of his neck. Naturally, I clung tighter. After alternately swimming and thrashing about, he managed to knock me off his back.

I recall being sucked down by the swift current, gasping for air and struggling desperately to get above the raging current. Just as I was about to lose consciousness, a brilliant white Light surrounded me in a protective bubble of oxygen and peace. With one enormous push, an invisible hand shoved me so that I hit the bottom step of the pier. With my last remaining strength and consciousness, I slowly pulled myself up, step by step, until I was above the water and on the pier. Once again I was visited by the brilliant white Light, but this time I was so close to unconsciousness I was not aware if the beautiful being came with it or not. My life had been saved by the Light; that much I knew, because Karl was not in sight.

Montreal held many adventures for me, from the childish pranks of holding up elevators in office buildings while workers buzzed impatiently to get on, to my first introduction to school after our arrival in a foreign country. The memory of being asked a question by my peers and answering "yes" and then "no" amidst growing jeers and laughter brought forth a determination not unlike my desire to see that Christ-like being in the "flesh." After that first introduction to my classmates, I resolved to not only learn the English language, but to master it so no one would ever know it was not my first or native tongue.

I had to really knuckle down and study because my English was limited to two words: "yes" and "no." I was given the option of sitting in on a fourth grade session in the afternoon (the first grade session only lasted until noon). I eagerly accepted the afternoon session and while everyone else merrily rushed home, I sat and listened to that new language so I could speak it without being laughed at. After two years of being behind my grade level, I was given the third grade curriculum one summer and, passing all the tests, was finally enrolled in fourth grade, which placed me in the proper class year. (I had already completed one year of school in Europe, but the language barrier forced me to repeat the grade.)

Once in my grade, I sought to help others with similar difficulties. I was asked to help an Italian girl who knew a few more English words than I had known but who was three years behind her proper grade level. The teacher could not communicate with my friend so I coached her during tests as well. I felt a smug complacency in my position of authority.

I experienced the usual emotional surges that accompany a human being's maturation process. In my case, however, I could only allow myself the liberty of experimenting outside the home. My parents were in such a dysfunctional, destructive relationship that I eagerly snatched and utilized any freedom at school or with friends. The world at large, both inner and outer, became my playground, and I eagerly sought to play and learn.

Karl's job allowed for little financial advancement so once again we packed up and moved to begin a new life in the United States. My years in Seattle were fairly uneventful, except for a few experiences. I had read books on hypnosis and other subjects related to psychology in an effort to make sense of my parents' behavior and to try and help them if I could. My first hypnotic subject, who was also ten and my friend, was not very receptive. I allowed myself one failure because it was my first half-hearted attempt. I knew, however, that if I really wanted to try again, I would succeed in hypnotizing a receptive subject so I put these experiments on hold.

While in Seattle, I grew very fond of a twelve-year-old boy in our neighborhood who had a reputation with the girls but was quite a rebel. Doug and a group of other boys would set up tents in the courtyard of the apartment complex and girls would flock in, whisper and giggle a lot, and emerge fifteen to twenty minutes later to be replaced by a new batch. Because I was not consciously sexually oriented then, I only dared to watch from a distance but I picked up on the clandestine sexual vibes issuing from those occupied tents.

Doug and I had a different ritual that we played out daily. He would ride his bike by, wave, and flash me a most flirtatious and mischievous manly grin while trying to keep his latest girlfriend from toppling off the handlebars as he rode by. I would smile and wave in return, my heart leaping to my throat. I definitely found Doug attractive, but my parents would have teased me for years had I engaged in any liaisons with him. This was not appealing to me so we continued our daily bike ritual and ventured no further.

One day I didn't see Doug ride by. I asked a friend about him. "Don't you know?" she said. "He died of a brain hemorrhage in the hospital last night. He got in a fight and the other kid knocked his head on the cement and he had a brain hemorrhage!"

My little world of pleasurable excitement and young love shattered. I couldn't cry because my parents would want to know why I was crying. They would throw Doug in my face in their perverted fashion so I simply stuffed my emotions. It was not until eight years later that I was able to face and release that pain. Fifteen years later an event would dramatically confirm my belief in reincarnation.

Within two to three years it was time to move once more. This time Karl's work took him to Alabama. My memories of that time are fairly uneventful, except for three experiences that again brought me face to face with the strange and/or supernatural, psychic worlds.

The first unusual experience occurred while I was baby-sitting two brothers, aged ten and eleven. Though I was only eleven or twelve myself, everyone always thought I was much older, so I got the job. While talking with the boys, the subject of hypnosis came up. The older boy said, "I bet you can't hypnotize anyone."

Not one to back down on an intellectual dare, I replied, "Oh, yeah? Bet ya I can!" not really taking it too seriously. When the time of reckoning came, I had to do my stuff. Picking the younger boy because he seemed to be a more receptive subject, I induced what I thought was a mild trance state in him.

It soon appeared that he was in a deeper trance then I realized. I asked him to walk across the room and shake his brother's hand. He did so in a somnambulistic fashion, with closed eyes and a gait not unlike that of a

Frankenstein creation, stiff and slow, like a zombie. His outstretched hand was also stiff and, curiously, colder and clammier than I would have expected. I enjoyed his older brother's wide-eyed look (That'll teach you to dare me!), and had the younger brother lie back down on the couch. Since he was in such a receptive state, I asked him about school, the subjects that he had difficulty with, and gave him a few positive suggestions for academic progress. I then told him he would sleep for fifteen minutes and wake up feeling much better. I never took another job baby-sitting those boys again, fearing that they would spill the beans over the unusual entertainment I had provided.

The second experience also occurred in my twelfth year. Karl began behaving more strangely, telling us that the Nazis were after him and were bugging the house. He was so convincing that when I found some loose strips of wire lying in our back yard, I thought he was right. It was much later that we discovered that Karl had been in Hitler's army so there was a semi-logical basis for his paranoia.

His behavior deteriorated rapidly. He became quite catatonic and spent hours sitting on a chair, gazing at one corner of the ceiling. My mother had to hand-feed him because he could no longer feed himself. Throughout the next two weeks my mother continued his feedings, unable to face the reality that the source of our bread and butter could no longer support us. Fortunately, a couple of my mother's friends told her to take him to a hospital for treatment. They stopped for gas en route to the hospital. Karl sprang from the car and pressed a twenty-dollar bill into the bewildered gas station attendant's hand, screaming, "Help, help! They're kidnapping me! Call the police!"

With a wave of their hands, my mother's friends indicated his mental state and the attendant returned the twenty-dollar bill. Needless to say, they made no more stops before the hospital.

Karl didn't come home for two and a half months so we visited him in the hospital. A man who closely resembled a survivor of Dachau, Karl shuffled slowly down the corridor toward us. His skin hung in limp bags from his emaciated face and body, which once had been amply padded. He was at least thirty to forty pounds thinner. His gauntness and slow, shuffling gait brought tears to my eyes. No matter what he had done to us, he didn't deserve this.

I resumed my psychology studies, desperately poring through Freud, Jung, and Adler, seeking answers for the tragedy that had befallen us. Karl was diagnosed as paranoid-schizophrenic, given forty electro-shock treatments, and released a few weeks later with massive doses of Thorazine and other anti-psychotic medications. Six months later he returned to work.

Because he took great pride in his role as "breadwinner," Karl always provided for us and made sure we were never homeless. Social programs such as welfare were far beneath his pride, and he struggled to support us at all times.

The third memory revolves around a dear friend of mine, Charles. He was one of my few friends who was not an adult. We shared the same classes and often met at his house, or stayed after school to play chess and talk about our lives, the world, the universe. We had many deep and absorbing discussions. It was difficult to find someone my age with whom I could communicate on this level.

One summer afternoon, shortly after lunch, my mother and I heard a neighborhood dog howl piteously for ten minutes. We heard no sirens and the dog did not sound as though it was in physical pain. My mother said that a tragedy occurred in the dog's family. Knowing that she often sensed when one of our relatives died before we got official word, I wondered what this meant. It did not take long to find out that, once again, I lost the only male friend of my age.

Charles and his brother, Dave, had been riding Dave's motorcycle. Dave thought he could outrun the train at a railroad crossing. His immature judgment resulted in serious injuries for him and cost Charles his life. The train hit the bike in the rear, where Charles sat, catapulting him ten to twenty feet into the air. He landed head first onto the cement, crushing his skull.

I went to the wake and wondered at the custom of theatrically disguising lifeless, traumatized bodies to make them appear as though they were simply sleeping. This is a barbaric practice. The physical body is a mere shell, clothing the soul drops when it's time to move on.

As I stepped up to the casket and looked at Charles' lifeless body, I "saw" Charles above the casket, smiling and dancing, happy to have gone on. I telepathically told him I did not think it was fair that so many "good" people died. I felt I should be able to go, too.

He merely kept on smiling and dancing as though to say, "It was my time, and I'm happy to be here. See ya later!" As I looked around the room, everyone was crying. I felt alienated. I couldn't cry because I had seen Charles and knew that he was happy. The mourners would not understand if I explained this, so I left the wake.

The funeral services were held at a local Catholic church, and my family and I attended. As I sat in a pew behind Charles' mother, his recuperating brother, and his father, I tried to pay attention to the service. My thoughts and feelings were pulled elsewhere, however. As the priest droned on in Latin, my inner voice said that Charles's mother would die of a heart attack in two months because no one had properly educated her concerning

Charles's soul and consciousness now that he had physically "died." The priest's droning created the seeds of a second tragedy, compounding the tragic loss of her son. My inner voice was always correct in these matters, and I had to forcibly hold myself in the pew so I would not run up to the altar and throw things off in an attempt to stop this second, impending tragedy.

I have always felt strongly that pain and suffering are not necessary, but few could see cause and effect as I could. Nothing could be done to avert this death. Since I was only thirteen, Charles's mother would not listen to my advice so I said nothing. She died of a heart attack within two months. The strain of losing her son and the lack of true information or education concerning his existence and whereabouts were too much for her heart. Though I knew better than disbelieve what I had received, I wished that it was not true. Such information is often difficult to handle emotionally, especially in teen years.

A few years later, Karl's desire for job advancement led us to the northeastern part of the U.S. I enrolled in a high school more academically advanced than the school I had just finished. After a few scheduling adjustments, I was "on track" once more and classes again became routine.

Chapter 2

A Different Adolescence

I began reading books on meditation. The *Autobiography of a Yogi* by Paramahansa Yogananda inspired me to meditate daily in an effort to keep my sanity amid the growing discomfort of teenage growth spurts and the increasing emotional disturbances within our family unit.

I was not popular with my peers and noticed that most of them had difficulty meeting my eyes when communicating. Although I was very well known and liked by the principal, school psychologist, school social worker, nurse, guidance counselors, office staff, and many faculty members, my peers did matter. Wondering what would make them so reluctant to make eye contact with me, I went home and looked in the mirror. Two laser-beam type eyes flashed back at me; I understood why few wanted to meet my eyes. Not wishing to be weird or different, I worked hard at camouflaging my eyes until they looked more normal. Looking at those eyes in the mirror made *me* uncomfortable—they were piercing and lacked a certain "human" warmth.

The more I meditated and did "inner work" on myself, the more alienated I felt. Strangers on the street often turned around to look at me as I rode by in a car. Store patrons stared at me at the end of an aisle, as though I had just been beamed down from a spacecraft. I wore typical clothing and did nothing to attract attention. It was unsettling. These reactions undermined my self-confidence; they corroborated my mother's perception that I really was "weird."

Family life and self-evolvement are antithetical to each other. I seriously considered quitting high school, moving out of my parents' house, and getting a job. The school "big-wigs" got together and told me they would help me get scholarships so I could go on to college. That was where I should be, according to them.

In January of my sixteenth year, my inner voice asserted itself once more. I had just finished drama auditions for Arthur Miller's play, *The Crucible*, which our high school was performing that year. At 4:30 or 5:00 in the afternoon I was walking home from school. A car with five young men in it screeched into our school parking lot, let one young man out, and peeled out of the lot and up the hill to the main road.

As I walked up the hill, my inner voice urged me to watch this young man as he disappeared into the woods to my right. By the time I reached the main road and crossed the street, my inner voice said, "Go to a house. You are being followed, and you will be attacked!" Thinking that I was hallucinating from meditating too much, I decided to slow down when I came to my turn, that the footsteps far behind me would just keep on going.

I had barely turned left onto my street when there was a sharp swerve in the footsteps and a marked increase in their speed. As the young man approached me from behind, his violence and hatred overpowered me, knocking me out of my body while he was still at least fifteen to twenty feet behind me. At that instant the light in my head went out. My inner voice said, "Now do you know the state many beings on this planet are in?"

The emotions that surged through me from the cessation of light and the words of my inner voice are indescribable. Physical death would have been nothing compared to this state of "no light" within my head. Suddenly, a loud cracking noise brought me back into my body. I watched as blood dripped onto my shoulder and realized I was being attacked. Another blow came, and then a third, before I could muster enough presence of mind to scream.

Ironically enough, screaming was just what we had been practicing at the auditions earlier. Although my voice was a little hoarse, my screams scared the young man, who ran back onto the main street. As I turned around, the same car I had seen earlier stopped to pick him up. It sped away with all five young men in it. Evidently, they were going to knock me unconscious, drag me off for a gang rape, and probably kill me later.

I staggered to the front porch of the corner house and rang the doorbell, blood dripping all over the concrete steps. The lady who answered the door took one look at me and after a brief explanation from me, hustled me into her house and called an ambulance. My mother was in the hospital for a hysterectomy and I didn't want to bother my stepfather, who already had his hands full. The kind neighbor insisted that because I was a minor, I could not get treatment. I called Karl.

The ambulance arrived and took me to the hospital, where I received a number of stitches. I was interrogated by a detective who thought I had fabricated the event. "Are you sure you weren't in a street fight and don't want your parents to know?" he growled at me.

"Do I look like the type who would get in a street fight?" I shot back. (At the time I looked like a typical bespectacled egghead or "nerd"—far from the then-current gang-type appearance.) I told him I could get character references my arm's length, beginning with the high school principal, all of whom would testify to my behavior and school record.

Nothing ever evolved from this attack, except a major brain concussion and a sense of outrage that I had been singled out as a victim so unjustly. It took three weeks before the severe nausea and dizziness dissipated. The fear of someone walking behind me and my habit of turning around to let them pass took two years to heal. It was not until many years later that I forgave the unidentified attacker. Life taught me that there are more expansive reasons for what I perceived as injustice. This was not my last experience of dangerous walks, however.

The following January, near the anniversary of my attack, I was suddenly seized by an overwhelming fear that I would be attacked once more. The inner voice simply said, "Don't worry, nothing will happen to you, but in three days, be careful." I blithely went about my business.

On the third day, I found myself walking in another part of town (which, I might add, was not known for violent activities) at dusk. As I was about to walk up the hill crossing a parkway, a car stopped on the other side of the overpass. A young man carrying some type of package ran into the bushes to my left. My inner voice had warned, "…in three days be careful." I watched this young man as he tried to disappear behind a bush. He eyed me rather nervously as I continued walking up onto the overpass.

Suddenly, the young man darted from the bushes and ran down the hill, as though toward the parkway underneath. My instincts indicated that I should cross the overpass and I did so, continuing at the same pace. When I reached the midway point on the overpass, the young man jumped over the fence at the spot where I would have walked had I stayed on the other side of the street. Surprised to see me across the street instead of on the side where he had hurdled the fence on the overpass, he began yelling loudly and tried to cross the overpass to catch me. Thanks to the traffic and my head start, I ran as fast as I could and evaded him entirely.

Another time that I escaped injury and possible death was on my way home from a trip to New York City. Eastbound from Manhattan, the train lumbered through one stop after another and the passengers thinned out more and more until I began noticing something strange. A young sailor who had boarded at Grand Central eyed me at every stop, as if to see whether I was getting off. The train pulled up to the darkened platform at my stop at approximately midnight. I got out and the sailor rushed out ahead of me. I knew I would not get a ride home so I was about to take a shortcut through some dimly-lit side streets. Then I suddenly decided that I would take the main road, which was brightly illuminated.

Coming down the stairs from the platform and entering the street, I saw no one in the murky environment. I began walking and reached the main street. Once I was on the main road, a strange fear swept over me. Thirty feet ahead of me, I saw a bright flash of light coming from some bushes to the right of the sidewalk. The street light evidently reflected off a metal object in those bushes, and I was not taking any chances. Immediately, I stepped right onto the main road. With cars honking and whizzing by, I continued walking on the street. When I passed the street light and reflective bushes, out jumped the young sailor, and off I went on a fifty-yard dash. I had a head start and attracted attention by running down the road instead of on the sidewalk. The sailor abandoned his prey. I was never so happy to get home to my parents' house as I was that night.

Toward my senior year in high school, I left home and moved to the "Big Apple" where I commuted seventy-two miles daily to and from school. Upon graduation, I began a summer job in the city.

Moving from Manhattan to the Bronx brought me many experiences typical of New York City life. I rented a room in a large brownstone near Fordham University. The owner of the building was a retired New York City cabbie by the name of Walter. He was a die-hard alcoholic and independently wealthy. Walter and I became good friends and he offered to teach me how to drive.

On my days off, we would play chess and talk. Weekend nights he would knock at my door at 3:00 or 4:00 in the morning and ask if I wanted to go for a drive. Never one to refuse an adventurous prospect, I would eagerly call out, "Sure!" and jump into my clothes. Ten minutes later we would be on our way to the Catskill Mountains.

Walter usually made me drive during the day, under very grueling conditions. Often we went "bar-hopping" before leaving the city. He would let me drive down a city street and then suddenly say, "Pull in here. I need to get a drink," when we were already twenty feet past the bar. I would find a place to turn around, park, and into the bar we would go. He would have his usual scotch and I would have my usual orange juice. When he'd had a few drinks, I would tell him it was time to move on and off we'd go until he spied another bar. It usually took between three and five visits before we ever got out of the city. By then he would be so inebriated that he fell asleep and I would be driving on my own.

I enjoyed the freedom and the responsibility of learning to drive with Walter. Handling a dysfunctional older man was old hat to me. With the help of another female renter, I would often put Walter to bed. She also felt sorry for him when he would stumble home alone and pass out on his bedroom floor.

My life in Manhattan and the Bronx left me with many adventurous memories and dangerous experiences. Once, when on one of my routine driver training sessions, Walter asked me to pull up across the street from a bar in Queens. He wanted me to wait in the car because he was only going to drop something off for a friend. While parked facing the wrong way on a one-way street, I noticed two men pull up and enter the bar carrying long black cases. No sooner had they entered than Walter rushed out screaming, "Let's get out of here, now!" He slammed his foot down over mine on the accelerator and we careened up the one-way street in the wrong direction. The two men with black cases ran out shortly after. Unable to follow in the same direction, they screeched around the corner.

Walter yelled, "Make a right! Turn left!" With the two men in hot pursuit, our high-speed chase took us through two or three boroughs before we finally lost them or they simply gave up. Little did I know that Walter's independent wealth came from shady dealings with Mafioso types.

Before I met Walter, I answered an ad for a rental on the Upper East Side of Manhattan. The man who answered the door seemed amiable enough, so I entered his apartment to see what he was renting and whether it had a separate entrance. He informed me that the room was at another location and propositioned me with an offer to be a Park Avenue call girl for him. He assured me that the clients were strictly non-local wealthy businessmen. When I wanted to leave, I found that he had locked me in. The only way I could get out was to talk my way out. He offered me a drink and I accompanied him to make sure he would not slip anything into it because he was interested in seducing me.

After two to three hours of verbal chess, he finally let me out of his apartment. Upon returning to my place, there was a message from him asking me for a date that weekend. I could not believe his nerve!

There were a few similar episodes with other men and it made me wonder how many young women fell into these traps, especially if they were homeless minors. New York City, one of the largest cities in the world, has a place for everything and I experienced some of its seamier sides.

Fall came, and I bid Walter "thanks and *adieu*." I had been accepted at the state university on a scholarship and grants. I couldn't turn down an opportunity of a lifetime for an education. Little did I know then the types of adventures that awaited me on the campus of a conservative state school in an Air Force town.

During my freshman year, I walked to a K-mart-type of store one evening around 6:00. As I trudged up the road from the campus, a young man approached me and asked me what time it was. As I answered him, he fell in step next to me, breathing quite heavily and clenching and unclenching his fists inside his pockets. I quickly scanned him to determine what psychological approach to use to prevent him from becoming violent. My instincts guided me to talk about brothers and sisters and non-threatening family life topics. This allowed me to keep him mentally occupied answering questions while we got closer to the store. Once there, I walked in with the strange man still beside me, pulled a pair of pants off a rack, and walked straight to the ladies' dressing room. For a moment, it appeared as though he, too, was coming in with me but fortunately he stopped just outside the dressing rooms.

"Do you know if there's a back way out of here?" I asked a customer, who eyed me questioningly. "No, it's not that," I continued. "I'm being followed, and I'm afraid the man will attack me if I don't leave without his seeing me." The lady went out front and was quickly followed by a saleslady, who listened to my story and told me she would be right back. Less than five minutes later she reappeared.

"The store manager is in front of the dressing rooms. His name is Jim so you can just walk out as though you were old friends. He will see that you get home safely."

"Thank you very much," I said with great relief, and walked out to meet Jim.

The breathless stranger was nowhere in sight. Jim walked me out, where I called a cab from a phone booth in front of the store. As I looked around, there was the stranger in another phone booth gesturing very violently. Suddenly, he snapped the receiver off the phone and stormed out of the booth. Witnessing that demonstration, I realized how fortunate I had been.

Before the cab came, Jim informed me that I was very lucky to have made it this far. Two girls had been raped in the store's back lot in the past two weeks. Whether it was the same man or not, no one knew, but judging from his modus operandi, it was best to take all precautions.

The next day I informed the Dean of this experience and Jim's statement and suggested that she put a warning notice on cafeteria and dorm bulletin boards, but she never did. Two or three more girls were raped within the next two months, but no one ever identified the rapist. I often wondered how many lives were ruined and careers seriously jeopardized as a result of the *laissez-faire* attitude of that administration.

Chapter 3

From Psychic to Mental Inpatient

During my freshman year, I began seeing a university psychiatrist (a mid-sixtyish European and classical Freudian) in an attempt to work though my emotional issues about my parents. I felt he should be sufficiently qualified to help me gain insight into myself and my life as a child.

During one session with him, he said, "I think you're rejecting your femininity because you do not wear dresses."

The Father of Psychiatry would have been proud of Dr. Polynski. I, however, was not. His statement elicited a challenging reaction in me. He frequently hurried to throw a door open for anyone in a skirt or dress. His diagnosis seemed most superficial under these circumstances. I bided my time until I could prove to myself that he either professionally knew what he was talking about, or he simply did not. I majored in psychology and had an extensive six-year background of my own reading in the field. My testing opportunity presented itself, but not until my sophomore year.

In the meantime, I further endeared myself to the administration through another series of encounters with the Dean and other administrators. I had a sophomore friend, Li-Yu, who was a whiz in computer science when it was still in its infancy. As we spent more time talking, she revealed that she had been a hooker before coming to the university. After hearing about her childhood, I certainly could understand why. She also intimated that if it were not for her education and future professional prospects, she would have had to return to that life.

The university had a number of rules, one of which was that all freshman and sophomore students had to spend every night in the dorms or they would be expelled. Juniors and seniors were exempt from this rule. Li-Yu was a sophomore, and I was a freshman so we both had to adhere to the rule.

Li-Yu's boyfriend was a junior and he had an off-campus apartment. One night she stayed at his apartment because he was emotionally upset about something and she wanted to help him. No sooner did this occur than she received notice that she was going to be expelled from the university. Always having been a champion of the underdog, I went to try to arrest the march of history in the Dean's office.

"I can name at least two girls from my dorm who regularly spend a night or two outside the dorms at least once or twice a week," I said. "It's interesting that they're not being expelled. Could it be because they're not Chinese?"

I brashly tried the same tactics on other administrators but Li-Yu was expelled, and my file was red-flagged to that of troublemaker.

At the onset of my sophomore year, I was surprised to find the two-story dorms replaced by ten-story towers housing three hundred and twenty students each. Upon entering my assigned room in these new towers, I was delighted that the roommate I was scheduled to live with was not coming after all. I had the room all to myself. What a great opportunity. I could open my room as a study room for any of the girls on the floor. There were two girls to a room, eight rooms to a suite, and four suites to a floor, which meant there were thirty other girls whom I could get to know through this potential arrangement. I had it made! Not only did this prove untrue, but other events that year cured me of my desire to complete my education at that university.

I found what I believed to be a novel method of testing Dr. Polynski. During one office visit, I decided to see how much he really knew about psychiatry. I began commenting about the moving colors in the room and on the walls, making remarks about his behavior and life style (into which I had psychic insight). Sadistically, I watched him squirm and puff nervously on his cigar. In retrospect, I wanted someone to see me, to understand my motives and feelings. Unfortunately, Dr. Polynski was not astute enough. My realistic impersonation of a psychotic convinced him that I was not simply neurotic; he became convinced that I was severely out of touch with reality.

Soon after my arrival at school that year, the university decided I needed a roommate. Everyone else had one, so they sent Janet, whom I had known from my freshman year, for a get-acquainted appointment. If anyone was a borderline psychotic, she was. One did not oppose official rules, however, so Janet came to see if we would get along as roommates. As she spoke of her likes and dislikes, I knew I did not want her as a roommate. Being direct with that administration, however, would lead nowhere.

I told Janet that I was sure we would get along fine, as long as she could tolerate my idiosyncrasies. Naturally, she wanted to know what they were. "Oh, you'll wake up in the morning, and my bed will be facing a different direction to coordinate with the moon's polarity with Venus, and Mars conjuncting the Rays of Saturn at certain degrees..." Her eyes widened perceptibly. "But I'm sure you will get used to it. I don't make much noise when I move the bed."

Janet was only too glad to leave my room and I was satisfied. She would not want me for a roommate, of that I was certain.

The two girls next door to me, Nancy and Evi, were quite creative and we shared a common unorthodox streak. We became good friends, and I began doing psychic experiments, teaching them to leave their bodies and journey into other realms. I planned to do a research paper on our psychic experiences so we spent much time together.

One day my inner voice said, "Lie down. You're going on a trip." Life had slowed to a dull roar, and this was just the thing to pep it up. Nancy decided to accompany me on this trip (All of my "trips" and work in this field are always done without the use of drugs or alcohol. These are sacred journeys and should be embarked upon consciously). She was not ready and I said so. Unable to really stop her, however, I let her use the empty bed in my room.

Within one to two minutes of accompanying me on this out-of-body journey, she screamed, "The light! The light! It's too bright! Oww..."

Too blunt for my own good, I said, "I told you not to go. You'd better return." At this point she did, and left the room. I continued on for a period of six Earth-time hours.

Three quarters of the way through, I reached a point at which The Voice spoke: "My child, you have a choice. If you wish to go on, you may do so, but you cannot return to this present physical vehicle. If you do not, you must return now!"

I felt as though I were at least five hundred miles away from my physical body. The heartbeat in my body quickened rapidly, then suddenly reversed and slowed. As the heartbeat grew slower and slower, I agonized over my decision. Looking back to Earth, I tried to find a tie, a reason for returning. No one needed me. I did not need any particular person, and no one loved me or had a hold on my emotions. There was nothing in particular I wished to accomplish, so there was really no earthly reason I could see to return. And yet ... as I searched for help in making this decision, I realized there was one thing I hadn't fulfilled. I didn't know why I was on Earth—why I was here.

I can't make this decision consciously; I don't have enough data, I thought. I'll leave it up to my soul, let it decide for me! The beautiful, peaceful yet ecstatic vibrations and tones abated as the Heavenly State I was about to enter fully receded before me. Upon returning to my body, I could not walk for three hours. I had grown a quarter of an inch, and the excruciating pain in my knees kept me off my feet.

This reaction wasn't the only bizarre result of my out-of-body experience. Much to my dismay, I found that I could hear thoughts in people's minds, word for word. Whenever I passed people on the street, or in the cafeteria, or sat near them in classrooms, I could hear their mind's incessant chatter. "I'm going to wear my new outfit for Fred." "This exam is taking forever." "Boy, was she good in bed."

I did not want this curse. I prayed and asked that it be taken away. I needed only enough insight to help others but not that much. Several days later, the ability mercifully receded.

The Saturday morning after my out-of-body experience, my inner voice woke me, urging me to get dressed at 7:30, an ungodly hour for a college student on a weekend. By 8:00 there was a knock on my door. The dorm director nervously asked if she could come in. Once inside my room, she said that she would like to take me to a doctor in town.

"Wouldn't you rather say a psychiatrist?" I queried.

"He's a doctor," she said awkwardly.

"All right," I said. "We'll play it your way, Rachel."

As we entered the emergency room of the local hospital, I saw Dr. Polynski. "How are you, Rose? Do you still feel the same way you did during our last visit?" he asked referring to my Academy Award-winning performance.

"Yes, with some minor variations," was my insolent reply.

Two large people walked into the room, a man and woman each weighing close to three hundred pounds. Hmmm, these two are here to see Dr. Polynski also, I mused. "No!" the inner voice shot back. "They've come to take you away!"

And with that, the woman took my left arm, the man my right arm, and cooed, "Come along, dear. We're taking you to a doctor on the outskirts of town." They physically moved me into a waiting sheriff's car outside.

After an hour and a half of riding in the back seat sandwiched between the woman on my left and the man on my right, I announced that I was shifting my position because I was getting cramped. The two bodyguards tensed, as though expecting me to jump through the wire-grated window separating the fully armed sheriff from us in the back seat.

"This is some outskirts of town," I muttered. The tension-charged atmosphere shifted to one of chagrin.

An hour later, the woman on my left thought, "That poor girl ... so young and ...

"Don't worry about me. I'll be out of here soon," I answered her thought.

She physically moved toward the car door. At that point, she was uncertain who was in need of mental help.

Arriving at Timberley State Hospital, I was stripped and duly dehumanized in the shower.

"She's got a birth mark on left upper torso, mole on right lower thigh..." The attendants prodded and poked to get all visible marks on their charts.

My civilian clothes were whisked away, replaced by standard state-issue mental hospital attire—dresses so long and large they gave the appearance of patients in *The Snake Pit*, though life at Timberley State Hospital resembled *One Flew Over the Cuckoo's Nest*.

The admissions staff apologized that they had no room for me and would have to place me temporarily in a ward with a hundred and fifty psychotic women. "It's only for a little while."

"Goddammit, she tied the ribbon on the rattlesnake, and the Archangel came down and God told her..." reverberated in my ears as I entered a room the size of a small auditorium. A middle-aged woman gesticulated wildly in mid-air with bony hands. I had arrived.

That evening, after being shown my bed in a vast hall of one hundred forty-nine other beds, I found it difficult to sleep, even with the lights off. Wails, low murmurs, and profane shouts drifted down the hall. As I was finally about to doze off, my eyes caught a movement near my bed in the dark sleeping quarters. A shadowy figure shuffled toward me with arms fully outstretched and hands poised to grab my neck. Not wishing to be a casualty on my first night, I whispered, "Look at the beautiful moon outside the window. Isn't the light bright?" and slowly slipped out of the bed on the other side. After telling the night duty nurse, the night stalker was given an injection, which halted her activities for the evening.

As the days went by, I grew more despondent. No one contacted me, and I had no link to the outside world. Within the first week, however, I saw a psychiatrist, Dr. Alvarez, who wanted to know why I thought I was in the hospital. After a thorough explanation of events, he asked if I would provide him with a synopsis of my work. Delighted to have some mental stimulation, I eagerly agreed. I brought it to him that week.

After examining my synopsis, Dr. Alvarez said, "Someday, when you are a famous psychiatrist, Miss Schneider, you can do this, but not now. You don't have a degree."

His grade in How To Win Friends and Influence People was an "F" as far as I was concerned.

I inquired whether I could call anyone at home.

"No."

Upon leaving his office, I went out to a pay phone on the grounds and called my mother collect.

"You sound so normal!" her half-hysterical voice sobbed.

"What the hell am I supposed to sound like?" I countered, anger rising.

"Did you do it? Did you really do it?" she asked.

"Do what?"

"Did you really strip nude, throw your clothes out of the tenth-story dorm window, and stand there naked?" By now her voice was gaining some composure, but I was quickly losing mine.

After inquiring who had told her that and hearing her say, "The university officials," I decided that enough was enough. I would take the necessary legal steps to get out of there as soon as possible. Fortunately, I didn't have long to wait.

Shortly after, I was asked to come to an attorney's office in the State Hospital. Upon hearing my story and asking a few questions, he said, "You don't belong in here, and I'm going to help you get out. You need to follow my instructions. The first thing is, don't tell your doctor anything. Let me handle it. Is that agreeable with you?"

It was only too agreeable. I eagerly accepted his offer. At last, here was one rational individual who believed me and would help me prove my sanity.

In the meantime, some of the psychiatric nurses noticed me working with a few of the patients. I was bored and trying to maintain my own sanity amid the daily screams, insane laughter, angry shouts, and wailing. Here was the perfect on-site training for a future psychiatrist/psychologist. One particular patient with whom I chose to work was Lori, a catatonic type in her late thirties. She did not talk and barely moved, so I began talking to her.

One day, I took her arm and led her outside for a walk as I was talking to her. She shuffled slowly but steadily beside me. Coming to the edge of one sidewalk, I thought that walking over the lawn would be a shortcut to where we were going. As I stepped off the sidewalk, Lori froze. Tugging on her arm elicited further resistance, so I tuned in to her problem.

"It's wintertime, Lori, and all the little insects and animals are underground. If you step on the grass, you won't hurt them."

Her stiff body relaxed, and off we went over the lawn.

These types of interactions interested some of the nurses. They often took me with them on their coffee breaks, plying me with questions on how I would respond to this patient or that patient. The day shift charge nurse, however, did not share their curiosity or enthusiasm.

Shortly after I had been admitted to the hospital, she introduced herself. "Hi. I'm Mrs. Forsythe, the day head nurse." Handing me a mop, she pressed it into my hands, saying, "You need to wash this floor. It's good for your recovery."

"Here, *you* mop the floor, lady! I didn't come here as a maid, I came here as a mental patient, remember?" I shot back, pressing the mop back into her hands. This teenage logic and audacity did not endear me in her eyes. She watched my behavior with extra care, hoping to catch me in some irrational activity so she could duly note it in her records. She soon found her opportunity.

I had been in Timberley approximately two and a half weeks. It was a deafening, smelly, and depressing environment. I needed some peace and quiet. None of the toilets had doors on them, our sleeping hall had a hundred and fifty beds, and the main hall was where we spent all our waking hours, except to occasionally go outdoors on the grounds. There was no privacy anywhere. One day I needed to release my stress before it completely overpowered me. I sat facing a corner of the main hall and simply allowed myself to cry until I had finished releasing my sorrows. This lasted three to five minutes, after which I felt much better. I sat for a few more minutes in that position, calming and centering myself within, and then got up and continued my day.

Soon after this episode, my attorney came through. Dr. Alvarez called me into his office. "Sit down, Miss Schneider. I understand you are going to court."

I nodded.

"Well, I thought I would share my feelings on the matter with you. I do not like the way these cases are handled in this country. In my country (Cuba) the doctor appears before the judge alone. In this country, the doctor and the patient both appear before the judge. But you're strong," he added patting my arm. "You can handle it."

I waited patiently for his next statement.

"Oh, there is something else you really should know," he continued, eyeing me closely. "If you lose your case, you will automatically be signed in here for a minimum stay of six months."

"Well, doctor, it looks like I have to take that chance, doesn't it?" I rose to walk toward the door. Suddenly, the full impact of his intent hit home. Turning and eyeing him coldly, I said quietly, "Gee, doctor, it's too bad you're not an American citizen."

Tears came to his eyes as he answered in an emotion-laden voice. "Please, please don't think that way!"

"I'm sorry, doctor, but you leave me no choice," I said coldly and walked out of his office.

The day of the hearing came soon after. Mrs. Forsythe had not forgotten me. The judge read her main clinical entry. "On the day of October twenty-third, patient exhibited extreme, bizarre, psychotic behavior."

"Obviously, your honor, breathing is considered 'extreme, bizarre, psychotic behavior' in this institution," I angrily interjected.

After reading a few more comments from the nursing staff regarding my interactions with other patients, the judge said, "Doctor, in your opinion, is this patient a threat to herself or anyone else?"

With eyes focused on the floor, Dr. Alvarez replied, "Your Honor, she is not."

"Then what the hell is she doing in here?" the judge shot back in frustration.

The doctor, still looking at the floor, replied, "Your Honor, I don't know."

The State Hospital wasted no time in releasing me. They allowed me to sign out on my own signature—a process not completely legal, since I was still a minor. In retrospect, however, I can see that they feared a multi-million-dollar lawsuit for wrongful confinement. They hustled me out as quickly as the university had hustled me in.

Returning to the towers later to collect my belongings, the dorm director physically barred my entrance. "Sorry, university regulations. We'll see to it that you get your things."

I asked if she would meet me at the local Howard Johnson's some time that evening. I was spending the night there and wanted to talk with her.

Rachel knocked on my motel door at 7:00 that evening and spent the entire night talking with me. When morning came, she thanked me for our conversation. "I can't believe all this happened to you," she said. "I don't understand how a university can get away with such things. In fact, I can't work with a system that allows these types of things to occur. I'm putting in my resignation." She was true to her word and moved on elsewhere.

I could write a complete book about my stay at Timberley, but that is not the purpose of this book. *One Flew Over the Cuckoo's Nest* is a very accurate replica of life at Timberley.

Recalling these memories still stirs some of the old emotions of anger and outrage, yet underneath and above these lies a deeper understanding. In many ways, I enjoyed my three-week stay at Timberley. I hobnobbed with people who were more responsive and psychically open than many of those walking on the streets. These were people with whom I could relate. Though their minds were more chaotic than those of the non-institutionalized, their hearts were often wide open and their visceral sincerity was refreshing. A spade was a spade, even if the handle looked like a snake. Figure that one out!

Chapter 4

From College to Black Magic

After being released from Timberley State Hospital, I had no place to go but to my parents' house. Once there, my frustration and rage at the injustice of life with them gave me another novel idea. I always felt victimized with them and I wanted to strike back or get even. Never one who could get even in a vicious manner, I searched for a method that would startle them and make them temporarily feel as emotionally unsettled as they had made me feel. Though my intent was to teach them a lesson, my real motive was one of revenge. I wanted to be emotionally vindicated.

The perfect method of revenge presented itself. I asked my mother if she had an old white cotton sheet that she did not want because I wanted to sew a nightgown for myself. Knowing that I hated to sew, she was puzzled, but she gave me an old sheet.

After laboriously sewing a nightgown, I placed several white candles around my bed and proceeded to lie down on it in my white sheet. My mother's curiosity had grown from the moment of my initial request. By the time I ceremoniously laid down on my bed with six lit candles around me, assuming a corpse-like position, her curiosity changed to shock, bewilderment, and then panic. These were all emotions she had aroused in me. Using my knowledge of psychology and acting abilities, I rivaled Whoopi Goldberg's performance in *Ghost* and my feelings were vindicated. But once again, I had failed to look at the potential consequence of my actions.

Two weeks after arriving at my parents' house and my performance in my white sheet and candles skit, my inner voice asserted itself once more. "You must leave today. Karl is having the sheriff and an ambulance come tomorrow morning to take you to Richmond State Hospital." Richmond State Hospital has an inmate population of thirty thousand, and I would have little chance of exiting once confined there. Knowing that I was in real danger, I took my sister, June, aside.

"June, I want you to listen carefully. I'm going for a long walk, and I don't know when I'll be back. Tell Mother I'm safe, that I'm okay. I'll be in touch with her soon. Please tell her an hour after I leave but not before. Okay?"

June nodded.

I hugged her and left. I walked to the train station and boarded a train for New York City. I wrote my parents a letter on the train and mailed it from New York City, knowing that was where they thought I had gone. I told them I was safe and not to worry, that I would return to visit again.

Instead of staying in the city, I returned to my college town, where I had a few friends who would help me. None of us had any money; I had to camp out in the woods. I spent four to seven days in the woods in the early part of November. As I huddled in a huge, heavy winter coat before a tiny campfire, my friends brought me food and much-needed companionship and support. The second night, the rain began. By the next morning, I was soaked through and through. I had no shelter other than the trees I was under.

That experience gave me first-hand knowledge of what homeless people endure. As I lay shivering under the trees, each drop of water hit me with the increasing impact of a sledgehammer. I came to understand the Chinese water torture. Though they were just drops of water, normally a life-giving substance, when soaked to the bone, each drop pounds your chilled, aching body with a life-extinguishing force. I withdrew and went deep within to find solace and help from spiritual sources. That eased the physical sensations of unbearable discomfort and probably saved my life. I didn't even catch a cold, although I lay in a dripping coat in a torrential downpour for two days.

Those were not pleasant times, yet they strengthened me. I learned much of the hardships some humans on this planet undergo. My friends collected some money so I was able to rent a small room for a week. I soon realized I had to return to my parents' house. I had no home, no job, and no money.

When I returned, my mother said, "It's a good thing you left. Karl had the ambulance and the Sheriff coming for you the next morning. They were going to take you to Richmond State Hospital."

My inner guidance had saved me once more. Once again, I found out that my mother had lied to me. Before I left, I had asked her if Karl was going to do that, and she had said no. By then, however, I was well-versed in their dysfunctional ways and was usually one step ahead of them—thanks to the guidance of my inner voice, which never failed me in dangerous situations.

My next stop on life's adventurous by-roads was in a small resort town in upstate New York. I spent the next ten years working summer and late winter there, and the fall and early winter working in Florida. During that time, I had a number of experiences which again puzzled me and raised questions regarding my sanity and my identity.

One of the first experiences occurred while I was working on the front desk of a large hotel, where I was being groomed to take on managerial duties. One day, while greeting a new guest, I saw his whole life flash before my eyes as I shook his hand. He was an alcoholic in the initial stages of liver trouble. He had three children, and so on.

This was too much psychic-ness so I asked for part-time hours, thinking I could get myself together sufficiently if I spent time on my inner life. This, however, proved to be only the first step in a series of events that finally took me to India several years later.

In the meantime, I began chanting "Om" in my spare time at home, mentally chanting it during all my waking hours, and even while I ate. Two or three months later, while resting in my apartment, an overpowering force rose from the base of my spine like a sledgehammer shooting out of a cannon. This sensation traveled all the way up my spine and ended in my brain, which throbbed and pulsed with an electrical energy I had never experienced before.

The force of it overpowered all other thought processes and as I looked inside to see what was occurring, I saw a huge fire inside my head. That image indicated a great electrical overload on the neural circuits in my brain, a rush of energy that had become trapped and needed to be released or polarized differently. As the pulsing sensation inside my head crescendoed into violent flames of electricity, I wanted to physically bash my head into the wall to stop whatever was happening. Instead, I called inward for help and instantly heard The Voice:

"Turn on a radio full blast and press it to your forehead."

I frantically clutched the radio, turned the volume as high as I could, and pressed it to my forehead. Instantly, there was an audible hissing, as though water were dousing a fire. All inharmonious sensations inside my brain ceased. It was my first Kundalini experience.

That fall some friends and I decided to go out west for a vacation. While in Albuquerque, New Mexico, we rented a house next door to ten people of various ages. While we were there, a young man from that house came to me for help because he had learned that I strongly believed in a God-Force. His plea for help was my most unusual experience up to that time.

"Can you help me? I can't get rid of her. She always comes to me and never gives me any peace," he said in great terror.

"Who comes to you? What does she look like?"

"It's her—she's half-woman, with the upper torso of a woman and the bottom half a snake. It's the Devil. He sent her."

"Why do you say that?"

"Because I was initiated. When I first came to them (the tenants next door), they told me I'd have to kill a baby and drink its blood in order to become part of their group. I couldn't bring myself to kill a baby, so I killed a puppy and drank its blood, and I became a member."

Life had shown me unusual scenes in the past, but none this unusual. My psychic sensitivities always gave me insights into many realities co-existing on this planet. Here was yet another to be studied. I tried desperately to help this young man. Nothing I could do in the limited time we had could help him. He returned to the fold next door.

The group was led by a Charles Manson-like young man who decided to invite his whole entourage into our house one night near midnight. (Evidently a girl we had befriended in New York, who had come with us on our trip, had invited the group over.)

"We're going to have a seance in your back room. Do you want to join us?" the leader asked me.

"No, thanks. I'm going to sleep." I was annoyed and turned over on the couch to sleep.

"You must go in there and stop them!" my inner voice thundered. Reluctantly, I rose and walked into the room, where all were gathered in a circle around a lit candle. They made room for me to sit in the circle and we clasped hands. I had never attended a seance before so I didn't know what to do. I sat in silence, watching the others, who seemed to be concentrating on something.

Searching the room to see what they were concentrating on, I saw that the candle flame was rapidly decreasing in size. There was no draft to cause this and I realized it was part of their process. My inner guidance indicated that I should not allow the candle flame to be extinguished, so I signaled my friend across the circle. She and I had worked on white Light in our prayers and meditations; she readily perceived what I wanted her to do.

Both she and I steadily visualized a brilliant shaft of white Light coming into the room. Within two to three minutes, the flickering candlelight shot up and maintained a strong, steady flame. There was a murmur in the room. The group broke the circle by unclasping hands. I finally went to bed and they returned to their house a few minutes later.

The next morning, my friend Judy said, "You know what happened after you left? A fourteen-year-old girl in the group said, 'Somebody was bouncing white light all over the walls. That's why we couldn't finish.' "

If Judy had had any doubts about the use of the white Light, that experience convinced her that the God-Light/God-Force is indeed omnipotent and can be used for much healing and good. Ostensibly, this group was going to bring back the spirit of a baby they said had died in that room, and they wanted to lay the spirit to rest. That was their version. In reality, I believe they had killed the baby in that room some time before we moved into the house. It was the one room I normally would never enter. I preferred sleeping on the couch to using that bedroom for myself. The vibrations in it were anything but peaceful.

Soon after that incident, the young girl who traveled with us awakened me at 2:00 in the morning, fearing for her life because they had threatened her at knife-point earlier. Fearing they would all descend on us in the middle of the night, we had to leave quickly. Three young women were no match for ten young men and women with a Manson-like leader who already hated me because I had tried to steal one of his male converts away from the fold.

Shortly after moving from that house, I met a chiropractor who was very psychic. He could clairvoyantly see auras and energies around people, plants, animals, and objects. Because of this gift, he was able to help many patients who had not been helped elsewhere.

One day, while talking with him, I asked him why he had a lock on the refrigerator, where he kept all his blood samples. He held up a vial of blood. "Can you see the beam of light from this vial and where it travels to?"

"No," I answered, "I can't."

"Then you're not ready for this work. Unless you can see where the light from this sample goes, you cannot do this type of healing work. The reason I lock up these blood samples is because there are ten thousand practicing Satanists in this town. They would just love to get their hands on some of these samples." (For those who are unfamiliar with this aspect of reality, those blood samples each had a connecting ray of light, of energy, to the person from whom they were taken. Practitioners of Voodoo, Satanism, and other forms of negative magic can do great damage to individuals by utilizing their blood samples in rituals. Hair, nails, or body excretions often are used as well, but blood carries a particularly potent life-link to the person and can thus be adversely affected by one who knows how to do this.)

The winter season was about to begin. We drove back to New York after our two-to three-month vacation of a lifetime. In the spring, I again went to Florida, and attended a meeting shortly after my arrival in Miami. A man whom I had never seen before, and who certainly had never met me, greeted me by name, saying, "Welcome, Rose. We've been expecting you."

I was a complete stranger, both to Miami and to all those at the meeting. No one had received an advance notice of my identity or likely attendance.

Soon after, my inner voice said, "You're going to meet a woman who will invite you to stay at her house for three days and two nights."

What a marvelous opportunity for adventure, I thought. And what an adventure it was.

I met the lady, another complete stranger, and accepted her invitation to spend time with her at her house. After psychically testing me, she offered me an equal partnership in an occult school she was planning to open. As I declined, she felt that she could at least persuade me, through occult means, by possessing me. When this attempt failed, she hastily threw me out of her house the next morning.

During another trip to Florida, I met a young man, Rick, who was eager to sever his ties with negative magical practices. Rick and I eventually rented a room with another young man in Orlando. While we were there one evening, his former teacher in negative magic slowly filled our room with one astral spirit after another, attempting to eavesdrop on my conversation with Rick. When the astral visitors became aware that they had been noticed and were asked to leave, she then employed stronger tactics to frighten Rick back into the fold. Directing a physical being to spy on us, she frightened Rick so much that, after seeing a man's face outside our window, he panicked. Running out the door with an iron bar in his hand, he yelled for me to come out.

The window we had been facing opened into a back alley. As I reached Rick, he gesticulated wildly at the ground. It had been raining just a few hours earlier and the alley was muddy. Rick's panic-stricken hands pointed to a single, fresh, naked human footprint in front of our alley window. There were no other footprints anywhere else. This one was quite deep, with five toes splayed, as though of a heavy man running.

"She sent a werewolf after me!" he whimpered in terror. Being fifty-one percent logical and left hemisphere dominant, I thought he was becoming somewhat hysterical in his assessment of the situation. It was rather odd to find one large footprint below our window after seeing a man's face briefly looking in on us earlier, though. I am aware that practitioners of certain occult arts are able to motivate and control energies and forces of which Mr. and Mrs. John Q. Public are entirely ignorant. I could not agree with Rick's assessment, however. There had to be a more logical explanation for this experience.

Soon after, Rick decided to accompany me back to New York. Shortly after our arrival, his paranoia peaked. One day while sitting in a friend's apartment, Rick was across the room from me, his back to a window, reading a magazine. I was about fifteen to twenty feet away, reading a cookbook. Much to my dismay, my inner voice interrupted a tantalizing recipe with alarming haste and brevity. "You must give him this message!" Knowing that these incidents occurred with some order of importance, I put down my book and turned to Rick.

"Rick, I need to give you a message I've just received. Some day, in the near future, you're going to be sitting with your back to a window, and it's going to be raining outside like it is now. You're going to want to commit suicide, and the reason you won't is because someone told you about this ahead of time so you'll know there is a God."

Feeling that I had relayed the message as requested, I turned back to my cookbook.

Rick's voice, trembling with paranoia and rage, broke the silence. "You're evil! You deserve to be killed, and I think I'll do it right now!"

Suddenly, he advanced toward me. Having a Black Belt in Karate, Rick could kill me effortlessly with one blow. Sizing up the fact that he was blocking the only escape route from the apartment, I surrendered within, in shock and dismay. I had been of service to this being, relaying a message that could save his life at a future date, and he was reacting with murderous impulses.

Silently, I prayed within. "Well, God, I did what I thought would be of assistance, and now he's going to kill me. Please make it quick. If it's my time to go, I accept."

Rick advanced to within six to ten feet in front of me. As I bowed my head, he stopped abruptly, as though he had hit a brick wall. Clutching his head, he whirled around and ran out the door, down the stairs, and up the street, screaming as though all the demons of hell were after him.

Raising my bowed head, I mentally said, "But, my God, I didn't want to hurt him."

"No, my child, you did not. It was his own evil directed back at him," came the instantaneous inner reply.

Several months later, I received a letter from Rick detailing the predicted event. He had been staying in a motel room and was sitting with his back to a window. It was raining outside. He was contemplating suicide when he remembered the prediction. This memory saved his life. He began believing in a benign Universal Force/Energy which loves all beings and Creation, and which most call God.

These incidents, and others, comprised a five-year period of my life when I was being schooled in the duality of the use of energies for positive, compassionate motives and results, and for selfish and/or violent motives and results. The latter is often referred to in occult circles as the use of "Black Magic." This term is in no way intended to refer to race or color or to imply racial discrimination.

Chapter 5

India and the Maharaji

W hen I was in my early twenties, my desire to go to India to
study the Yogis and find an "enlightened being" became
overpowering. I had little money and one day the inner voice
spoke during my meditation. "You will be going to India soon."

"Oh, yeah? And just how will I get there with no money—levitate?"
my logical mind snapped back.

"When the time comes, the money will be provided," the voice answered patiently.

Months before, I had let several friends know that one day I would
travel to India. They reacted very much as my own left hemisphere had.
"Yeah, yeah! We've heard that one before. Another one of her pipe dreams!"

Not long after this message, a combination of events occurred that
provided both the money and a platonic male companion, Fred, who accompanied me to New Delhi. I was in search of the Christ-like Being whom
I had met in the wheat fields behind the health spa. The memory of the
meeting was still vivid, even though the time was eons ago.

About a year before I went to India, I had met a religious leader from
India, Gopi Singh Khalsa, while in Florida. His teachings and meditations
so impressed me that I was determined to travel to India to see if he was as
charismatic and sage in his own country or merely performing on an adrenaline high in Florida. After all, I was searching for the Christ-like Being
whose behavior was not dependent on his external environment. Nothing
but the real McCoy would do.

In Delhi, Fred and I took a trip to Gopi Khalsa's ashram. We pulled
into the ashram just as his Mercedes passed us on its way to his mountain
ashram in Nainital. After a three-hour delay, we shared another taxi with
two others on their way to Nainital. Arriving in Nainital that night, we
barely got settled at the ashram when the 4:00 a.m. wake-up gong sounded,
signaling the time to meditate before breakfast.

Fred and I suffered from jet-lag, so we weren't in the best of moods. As
the morning wore on with still no sign of Guru Khalsa, I spoke to some of
his long-time disciples about my need to see and speak with him. A driven
Westerner unaccustomed to the Indians' utter disregard for time and cir-
cumstance, I grew increasingly impatient at the lack of communication.
The guru was nowhere in sight and with overt frustration, I explained that

I had traveled ten thousand miles to see him, and I would like to be able to do so that day.

My wish was finally granted. I was led to another building. The door opened, revealing Guru Khalsa and a handful of disciples, mostly women. After a brief exchange, I noticed that the guru was not as vibrant or wise as he had been in Florida. Determined to find out whether he was the being for whom I was searching, I psychologically baited him to expose his ego, if he had any (a truly Christ-like Being would not).

"Well, go to Rishikesh if you think you will find a holy man there," he sputtered in exasperation.

Fred and I boarded a bus that day and headed for Rishikesh, a small town nestled in the foothills of the Himalayas. Rishikesh is famous in India because the sacred Ganges flows by and it's a place of spiritual pilgrimage. It's full of ashrams and the center for Swami Sivananda's ashram, as well as several others, including one for Maharishi Maheshe's Transcendental Meditation (TM) students. In short, it is a "holy place" by Indian standards. Thus it was illegal to bring eggs, fish, or meat inside the town limits. Fortunately, this did not affect me because I was then a vegetarian in the true Yoga tradition. Fred and I were, however, affected by our ignorance of the two distinct parts of Rishikesh: the town itself and its spiritual center bordering both sides of the Ganges.

The first night in town, we slept in a hotel room (loosely termed) which resembled something out of *Ali Baba and the Forty Thieves*. The room had natural ventilation from above, plus the added feature of the most panoramic view of a night sky I have ever experienced while in a room. It also provided the local flavor of odors wafting through the night air from the drunks who would relieve themselves a mere ten feet outside our door. In addition, the door had no lock on it. Fred and I greedily shared the one thin woolen blanket I had mercifully thought to buy while in Nainital.

After pushing the bed against the door, we spent a very cold, fitful night, continually waking to the strange sounds of drunks and others shuffling by outside our door. Our adrenaline reached new highs with the occasional rattle of the doorknob or the door hitting the bed as one or more strangers attempted to gain entry to our room.

The welcome dawn spread itself like a shield of light across our faces, forcing the cold, uncertain darkness to retreat. We traveled to the other part of Rishikesh—the spiritual haven on the banks of the Ganges.

After making a few inquiries of some English-speaking Hindus, we were offered a room at the Shivananda Ashram, an improvement over our last one. We didn't get the panoramic view of the sky, but we certainly got enough fresh air through the iron bars in the window. Window panes are an unnecessary luxury, but the bars are an absolute necessity if you want to wake up the next morning—they kept the tigers out. In the 1970s, Rishikesh usually lost one or two people a month to the hungry tigers that would come down from the mountains in search of a meal.

Our stay at the Shivananda Ashram lasted about three weeks, during which time we gained a better understanding of the Yogis and other spiritual seekers. A few memorable events of that time come to mind.

I was surprised to learn there were thirty Russian scientists funded by the Russian government staying at the ashram. They, too, were studying the Yogis, but for very different reasons than those of most of the other "seekers." The Yogis' mysterious and phenomenal mind control over life-sustaining bodily functions was a subject of great interest to them. Because they added much-needed funds to the ashram's coffers, they were welcomed.

During our stay, we met a Swami who befriended us and shortly proved to be most instrumental in steering me to my goal. With each passing day, I had grown increasingly more despondent because each day meant I was that much closer to returning to the United States without finding the "Being of Light."

One day the depression reached its peak. As I stood on a boulder overlooking the Ganges, I gave God my ultimatum: "If I don't meet this Being soon, or in some way discover whether this search is real or not, I'm going to jump off this cliff!" Every cell in my body vibrated to this ultimatum.

That evening Fred and I retired to sleep. As I was about to lie down on my bed, a strange mist came through the bars on the window. The night was clear, with no fog in sight, so this mist aroused my curiosity and alerted my senses. I sat back up in bed, watching closely as the mist came horizontally into the room and suddenly gathered vertically before me in the shape of a man. Fred was also awake and observing this mist change shape from his bed on the other side of the room.

I had been involved in so many clashes with people practicing Black Magic before I came to India that my first reaction was one of defense. "Oh, no! Not in India, too! Now there's a llama from the left-handed (negative) path coming to challenge me!" I thought.

The Being before me cocked his head to one side. A large, visible question mark formed over his head and a questioning tone rang in my ears. The vibrations emanating from this Being were of the purest love and innocence I had ever experienced. I relaxed my psychic defenses. The shape before me dissipated, and the mist wafted out through the bars the same way it had floated in.

Turning to Fred in awe, I said, "I don't know what just happened here, but I think this is a significant event in our lives. And this is just the beginning!"

The following day, we were walking by the river when our Swami friend greeted us, asking, "So, how do you like India?"

"I love your country very much," I replied, "but we've been here three weeks, and I haven't met a Saint yet!"

"What, you have not met a Saint?" He was astonished and hurriedly fumbled through his pockets, pulling out two pictures. One was of a being called "Tattwalla Baba" who lived in a cave in the mountains above us.

I eagerly asked the Swami how we could visit this Saint. After learning that we would have to hire a group of about thirty villagers with kettles and other noise-makers to scare off the tigers, leopards, panthers, and other wild carnivores, I reluctantly decided to postpone this visit until a future time. Perusing the second photograph, I was startled to see that this Saint's face was familiar.

"Isn't that the man in the book, *Be Here Now*, by Ram Dass?" I asked Fred.

"Sure looks like him."

The Swami was only too happy to give us directions to Neemkerole Baba's ashram. That day we were on the train headed for Vrindavan, Lord Krishna's birthplace. We stopped in Agra and went inside the Taj Mahal, a most impressive palace, the inside of which has the best acoustics of any building in the world. There were signs requesting NO WHISTLING and NO SHOUTING. The slightest sound reverberated a thousand fold (it seemed) from every surface inside the palace walls. It was a magnificent echo chamber, the likes of which most people will never experience.

After spending one night in Agra, we continued on to Vrindavan. Finding the proper address, we knocked on the gate of an imposing twelve-foot high spiked wall around an ashram. When the gate opened revealing a Westerner in Yogic garb, we were asked if we had a letter of invitation.

"No," I said, surprised.

We were then asked where we came from.

Upon hearing "Rishikesh," the man said, "Just a minute," and closed the gate. Several minutes later he returned and opened the gate. "Ah, you must be the two people from Rishikesh. Maharaji's been asking everyone here for the last two or three days: 'Have the two people from Rishikesh come yet?' "

With that miraculous pronouncement, we were ushered into the ashram and invited to share a room with some Westerners.

We pondered the events of the last few days. It was only two or three days ago that the mist had appeared in our room at night, the Swami had given us directions to the ashram of Neemkerole Baba (or Maharaji, as he was commonly addressed), and we were on our way to see him. There were no telegraphs or phone connections between the ashram in Rishikesh and Maharaji's ashram in Vrindavan. It was an entire day's trip by train one way, so we were certain that no letters had been written. Besides, the gatekeeper asked us for our letter of invitation, so that left only one conclusion: the mist in our room in Rishikesh approximately five hundred miles away was the Maharaji. It was truly miraculous!

The next day we joined the other Westerners for Darshan (coming into the presence of the Guru or Holy Man/Woman). Maharaji spoke to a few Westerners through an interpreter and then, turning to me, motioned for me to come up to him.

As I approached, the purity, love, and light emanating from his auric field convinced me that here was the Being I had been seeking for twenty years. All questions disappeared from my mind. After asking me a few questions about my home town in America, he turned and, laser-like eyes searching my soul, said something in Hindi to his interpreter.

"You are very sharp," the interpreter said, translating Maharaji's words.

Suddenly, my mind went completely blank. I didn't know who I was, where I was—I couldn't even remember my name. There was only a vague memory that I even had an egoic identity. My mind frantically attempted to retrieve that identity. It took three hours of sitting alone in the desert to recapture it.

Maharaji had answered my lifelong question of "Am I insane?" His four simple words confirmed what my inner voice had always said, yet I could never emotionally accept. My mother had always told me I was either a genius or insane. Realizing I certainly wasn't a genius, I believed her other assessment. I never did fit in anywhere, so I feared that she was correct in her perception of my behavior.

Our stay at Maharaji's ashram was filled with adventure and miraculous events. Shortly after our arrival, I came down with a severe flu and a very high fever. I was so weak I couldn't walk. When the morning Darshan came, all the ashram residents ran over to Maharaji's compound, advising me to stay because I couldn't walk with them. An instinctive inner urge pushed me to half-crawl, half-stagger over to see Maharaji. When, as was often his custom, he touched my head, the fever and weakness instantaneously disappeared. I was elated, knowing that this inner force had led me to make the right choice, even though everyone around me tried to dissuade me from attending Darshan.

While at the ashram, Fred and I would take daily walks into neighboring areas. More than once, we heard local gossip that Maharaji was sexually promiscuous, a trait not compatible with the behavior of a "Saint" in India. It was said that after one woman left through the front door after intimacy with Maharaji, another would come in the back door. He would be sexually intimate with her and others as well. After hearing this, I was determined to find out for myself.

One day, when all my roommates had gone somewhere, I took the picture of Maharaji from the small personal altar that also had a picture of Christ, Maharaji, and Shirdi Sai Baba on it. Putting it on top of my head, I mentally thought, "Okay, old man, we'll see if you've truly overcome the personal passions as a true Yogic master has. We're going to find out whether you're being intimate with these women for their spiritual progress or your own pleasures."

The vibrations emanating from this picture would give me the answer instantaneously. I would get a headache from the picture if the answer was the latter.

A beautiful golden light cascaded around me from the picture on top of my head. A deep inner peace and love enfolded me. The Maharaji flowed with whatever was needed to raise another to greater spiritual awareness and growth. If sexual intimacy with a particular individual was in his flow, I accepted it as of that moment. As I put the picture back on the altar, my question was sufficiently answered. I left the empty room to have lunch.

At Darshan the following day, I wanted to ask Maharaji some questions about meditation and prayer. My prior psychic test and results were no longer an issue; I had forgotten all about the "closet" incident.

Maharaji could tell I wanted to ask him some questions. Gesturing to the others, he said, "*Jao*" (go), and motioned for me to come to him when all had left. As I approached him, he gently pinched me in the crotch and asked sweetly, "Now, what do you wish to ask?"

His action was the most asexual one of that type I had ever experienced. In one small movement, he had shown me that he was fully aware of what I had been doing with his picture the day before. He wanted me to know that nothing escaped his awareness. It was perfect! A verbal statement to that effect would not have had the impact of that one small gesture. It encompassed all levels of my question. My awareness of Maharaji's spiritual stature expanded. I then asked him about meditation.

Maharaji's omniscience was revealed at yet another Darshan. This was one of the rare times that Maharaji let Indians and Westerners come together for his Darshan. (He usually saw Indian people separately from Westerners.) That morning, Maharaji played his version of "Monopoly" with us. Turning to each of us individually, he would ask for a certain sum of money—thirty rupees from one, fifteen from another, and so on. As each handed him the money, he gleefully riffled through the growing stack like a small child playing. Turning to our American friend, Jack, who had invited us to share his room, Maharaji said, "Here is the twenty rupees you've been praying for the last ten days."

As he handed Jack the money, Jack burst into tears. No one had known about his need. He had prayed silently for the money and told no one about it.

Turning to an Indian woman in the crowd, Maharaji addressed her in Hindi and handed her a large number of bills. She, too, burst into tears. We eagerly asked an English-speaking Hindu what had transpired.

"She has just walked three hundred miles from her village to see Maharaji for his help and blessings. She told no one here that her son died, and that she has no money for the funeral. Maharaji just gave her three hundred rupees for it."

As Maharaji turned to first one, then another, saying a sentence here and there while handing them a bill or two, we saw the same emotional scenario repeated each time. Maharaji evidently knew how to speak to a person's heart, touching all more deeply and lovingly than they ever had experienced before. All had prayed and called to God in the silence of their hearts; all were answered by Maharaji. He was truly the remarkable Being of Light with whom I had played in the wheat fields as a child.

One evening, Fred and I wanted to get some chai (tea), but it was past the eight o'clock curfew. The gatekeeper normally would not let us back into the ashram once we left the compound after curfew. Fred persuaded him that we were "dying" to have chai so he opened the gate, promising to get us back in when we returned.

As we reached Maharaji's gate, a force began pulling on me from behind, as though someone was physically holding me back. Within a few seconds the pull became so strong that I was actually physically walking in place, unable to move ahead. I tried turning around toward the ashram and the force stopped. In defiance, I turned again and tried to forge on past Maharaji's gate toward the town. Once again the force held me physically in place until I turned back toward the ashram. Because I really wanted some chai, I stubbornly went through this charade a few more times before giving up.

Maharaji must have been trying to save us from some danger that evening or he would not have prevented us from going any further. Reluctantly, Fred and I returned a few minutes later to the surprised gatekeeper, who just shook his head at those "strange Americans" who leave for a planned hour or more, yet return hastily in three or four minutes.

The last memorable experience with Maharaji in India occurred the last day of our stay at his ashram. During my last Darshan with Maharaji, he telepathically communicated this message to me: "You will not see me in this physical vehicle again."

The message had a vibration of finality. He was telling me that he would leave his physical body soon after I left India (die, as we Westerners term it). True to form, my mind immediately analyzed this message. This is not a telepathic message but a rational thought because of his appearance of age. You're just assuming this.

Little did I know then how true his telepathic message was.

After eight weeks in India, Fred and I reluctantly returned to the States. We returned because he had had an ample supply of hashish and other hallucinatory substances readily available. I returned because my spiritual quest would now change direction once more.

Five months after our return, I was walking to work one day when Maharaji's loving presence enfolded me once more. I had not felt this since seeing him in India. I was so elated I felt as though I were floating ten feet above the ground. Though I didn't understand the reason for his visit at the time, my joy at this honor was unbounded. Two nights later I had the following astral experience.

I was facing Maharaji, who was flanked by five male disciples in loincloths. I wore a tailored suit. Maharaji grabbed me by the jacket's lapels, saying, "What is this?" meaning the suit I was wearing.

"If you don't like it, Maharaji, I'll take it off," I replied, wishing to please him.

He pulled me toward him so closely that we were eye to eye. "What do you want?" he asked gruffly.

"I think I want to follow you," I answered meekly, not wishing to incur any further disapproval.

"Then go!" he said, pushing me away from him. "The way is very dangerous and there are many wild beasts in the jungle along the way, but go if you must, and I will meet you on the other end!"

With that, I began walking away from Maharaji into the surrounding jungle as he remained seated with his five disciples still around him. The next morning, Maharaji's presence was gone.

The following month, I received a postcard from India. It was from the Swami in Rishikesh who had originally given us the address to Maharaji's ashram. The post card read, "By now you must have heard Maharaji went into Mahasamadhi (physical death) on October __."

That was exactly the day his presence enfolded me ten thousand miles away in New York State. So the telepathic message at the last Darshan in India was real. Maharaji knew of his upcoming departure from this plane and he wanted me to know telepathically. It wasn't my mind reasoning after all! Though I was relieved to know that, yes, I had received the message accurately, I was saddened by Maharaji's departure from this plane. I could not visit him in India again. Though I knew that Maharaji had made some "last minute connections" with me on the inner planes, it wasn't quite the same as being before a living, breathing, physical form you could touch and hug.

Life continued uneventfully until I had another astral experience one night several months later. As I was falling asleep, I was taken aboard a spaceship to a room with a large oval table. There were twelve seats around it, eleven of which were occupied by very tall, thin beings. I was invited to take the empty seat. After accepting, I was immediately asked, "So, what have you observed about Earth?"

As I replied, the eleven stately-looking beings conversed among each other.

After asking me a few more questions they again turned to me. "We are taking you back now. When the time comes, you will remember."

I sat straight up in my bed, saying aloud, "Remember what? I want to know now!"

I was unable to sleep for some time after returning from the ship. My mind raced, trying to find answers to this unusual experience. It was not until twenty years later that I was allowed to remember, thanks to Evelyn and her love and dedication to truth and spiritual advancement for all.

Shortly after this last astral journey I met my husband-to-be.

Chapter 6

Seeking Help

George, my future husband, was a musician romantically involved with a local negative witch who had an avid interest in necromancy. He and I became friends through a young man with whom I was then romantically interested. George and I saw each other once a week or more for about a year as platonic friends. I helped him see his one-sided relationship more clearly and taught him what to watch for in his girlfriend's relationship with him. (We discovered that she wanted George's virgin teenage son as a sacrifice for her Satanic rituals.)

A year later, his girlfriend found another lover/victim and George moved out west with me, primarily for his health. I began a job in an Arizona desert resort and began settling into my new surroundings. One day, as I returned to my room at the resort after the morning shift, the inner voice urgently said, "Call the Tolleson police!"

I had no reason to call the police from a neighboring town and was about to take a nap when someone knocked on my door. When I opened it, there was a note on the door that said, "Call the Tolleson police!" There was a phone number to call.

I did so and found out that George was so seriously ill with an asthmatic attack that a priest had given him the last rites. The police were trying to obtain his permission to let an ambulance take him to a hospital. Instead, he had them call me.

This was the beginning of a long series of such dramatic life-and-death struggles with George. I felt that, since we loved each other, I should help him all I could, so I stayed with him for about ten years. In that time, I was determined either to see him physically healed or to assist him in his transition from the Earth plane as harmoniously as possible. My experiences during the years I spent with George could fill a book, but I will only touch upon a few highlights here.

One of my memories revolved around the ice cream vending route I had at the time. George couldn't work because of his health so I took a job selling ice cream. I leased an electric cart from a small businessman who sold me the ice cream wholesale. One day, as I was driving in another part of town near the broccoli packing sheds, I went down a street I had never been on before. A row of migrant workers' shacks lined the street on one side, facing the vegetable fields on the other.

I drove slowly up to the end of the street, ringing the bell that indicated the "ice cream lady" had arrived. A few migrant children came out and bought some ice cream. They had gone back into their homes and the street was once again quite deserted.

As I turned the cart around and ambled back down the street, I saw a young boy. He appeared to be about eleven or twelve and as I approached him, the strangest feelings rushed through my body. I stopped the cart about twenty feet away from him. The young boy also stopped his approach and we simply stared at each other in amazement. I was a woman in my twenties who was suddenly experiencing full-blown sexual feelings and explosions of loving recognition toward an eleven-year-old boy! Evidently, the young boy was experiencing the same. As waves of energy passed between us, I couldn't bear it any more and drove away in my cart. I realized that these were the same feelings I had experienced with Doug some fifteen years before when he had been alive and we had both been the same age.

Here was Doug again in a young Mexican boy's body. Although this young boy did not physically resemble my first love in any way, the energy of recognition and love between us was unmistakable. It was so overpowering that the only way I could deal with it was to leave and never return to that part of town again.

I never saw the young boy again; he had to live out his life without me. That experience strengthened my belief in reincarnation. I now had first-hand proof of it in this lifetime. My rational mind is amazed and skeptical to this day, but my intuitive "parts" know with a certainty what only life experience can impart. I have always maintained that people may lie, but energies do not. I might add, for the benefit of other skeptics, that I have never before or since been attracted to younger men, much less boys less than half my age.

Another memorable experience revolved around my boss, the man who owned the ice cream company. Though I was an independent contractor, I still viewed him as a boss of sorts. One day, George asked me if I would attend an Alcoholics Anonymous meeting with him. I was not an alcoholic but I reluctantly agreed to accompany George because he had invited me. After all, one could always learn something from every experience.

Much to my surprise, I saw the owner of the ice cream company at the meeting. Once the meeting ended, we all drifted out into the hall. My boss and I were soon engaged in a conversation. As the conversation progressed, I suddenly became aware that I was speaking to him about death and dying and what happens to the spirit. The logical part of my mind was horrified. I had never spoken to this man before about anything except ice cream and business. Because of many similar experiences with others, however, I continued channeling this information. After educating him on the finer points of death and dying, we all said good-bye and went home. I had no conscious knowledge of the reasons behind initiating this most unusual topic with my boss.

About a week later, he called me on the phone. "I'm sorry to call you like this, but I didn't know who else to call. I've been having a lot of pain in my side, and I've been feeling nauseous for a day or two now. My brother says I should go to the hospital. What do you think I should do?"

My silent inner voice said, "He has cancer of the liver. He will die in three days."

I simply told him that his brother was probably right. It was the only place he could get a real rest from his daily affairs, and that would do him some good. He entered the hospital and died three days later of cancer of the liver.

I would like to point out that my logic is very strong in its skepticism regarding such intuitive and wondrous flows of life. After forty-some years of repeatedly witnessing such events, I still doubt. I must consciously put my "Doubting Thomas" to rest with each experience in order to allow the intuitive to flow freely. All of you who are also struggling with this, take heart. It's possible to open to your higher, or intuitive, self. It just requires an inner surrender once you have allowed this faculty to function, and you become familiar with it.

In response to those who may wonder why I did not simply tell my boss what I "heard," here is the reason: Most human beings with no meta-physical training or education are simply unprepared to deal with this type of information on such short notice. I rarely speak of the time of one's death—even with close friends who are dying. Additionally, if I do reveal this information, then I bear the responsibility to help them in their transi-tion from this plane. I do not accept that role eagerly in many cases. We each have our "specialties" of service in life. Helping others "cross over" from this physical plane is not one of mine. It's merely a service I perform when "The Flow" indicates.

There are numerous other types of experiences I could recount but I will not go into them. Suffice it to say that my years with George were filled with emotional, spiritual, and physical pain as well as ecstasy—an ecstasy derived from witnessing the "Divine" at work behind the scenes. In retrospect I can truly appreciate the beauty of that Divine Flow of Life. As for most beings on this Earth, the old saying, "Hindsight is better than foresight," most accurately applies to my life at times. (This is less fre-quently the case when one's intuitive foresight is both highly developed and trusted implicitly. That combination is rare and is one all spiritual seekers strive to attain.)

My life with George ended when he left the physical plane ten years after we vowed our love for each other. I had been his partner, nurse, caretaker, and spiritual guide all those years. At first I thought I had failed. He died, and I thought he could have been healed. I did not see then that healing takes place in many ways, on many levels. When a soul has learned all it can from the experience of an incarnation, it withdraws the Life Force from the physical vehicle and the body dies. George had reached that stage of his "healing," manifested by his leaving the physical plane. His spirit sought experiences and growth on other planes and dimensions.

My emotional reaction to George's transition was surprising because I had so much insight and information regarding the death process in general and his in particular. Being at least partially human, however, I experienced the full gamut of grief. It was a beautiful, bright, sunny day outside, yet all I could see was a dark wall of grief. As I wrestled with this darkness, a being in brilliant golden Light appeared before me, smiling from ear to ear. "You have done well," he said. "You have spared this being (George) two hundred incarnations."

The darkness suddenly crumbled as the bright Light penetrated me fully. A thousand-pound weight fell from my shoulders, and I thanked the God- Force. My years with George were worth it, after all. My time was not wasted; I had been instrumental in his spiritual growth. It was only then that I realized George had been healed.

I was physically weakened from the strain of caring for George, the drama of ten years of daily life-and-death struggles, and my own inability to adapt fully to the physical and chemical environment of this plane. Another ten-year odyssey began, much of it punctuated by daily survival issues and the responsibility of caring for a small child who had lost her father. The journey of single parenthood was not easy, but it revealed my true strengths and enabled me to deal with all vagaries of life. A challenging path, indeed, one where boredom rarely takes root.

After many years in survival mode, I grew increasingly despondent. I felt my Life Force weaken. I'd had many near-death experiences in which I consciously forced my heart to keep on beating when it threatened to stop. The stress of survival was wearing me down and in final desperation, I called to the Universe for help. Soon after my desperate plea, I picked up a copy of a local magazine that listed traditional and non-traditional therapists. The magazine fell open to the page with Dr. Fuqua's ad, and my eyes focused on her picture. I knew instantly that I needed to call her. The rest is history. Evelyn explains it quite well so I don't need to relate this story.

I do, however, wish to include the following. For a period of approximately twenty years, I had known that I would meet a woman who would help me find myself. I had attempted therapy with a female therapist on one other occasion. Although I believed at first that she was "the one," this later proved to be disappointingly untrue. By the time I met Evelyn, I had forgotten this by then insignificant detail.

It was not until six months after beginning hypnotherapy with Evelyn that I recalled this prescient information. Once again, I was awed by the synchronicity of life's journey. The perfection of such moments truly astounds one's mind and the wonder of it never ceases. All That Is is always many steps and dimensions ahead of our limited daily perceptions. I never cease to be amazed at the grandeur of Creation and the manifestations of its many forms and frequencies. My love and reverence for the All That Is is both unbounded and unspeakable in such moments of expanded vision.

In closing this autobiography, I would like to share the following message from Gehema:

There is a Light which shines so brightly that no human eye can fully perceive it; yet, this Light is all around us, through us, and within us. It is this Light which vivifies us and nourishes us. It is the 'Manna from Heaven' of which your Bible speaks. Open your vision. Open your senses to receive this Light and you will never lack for warmth, security, love, harmony, joy, or peace. For this is the Light of Truth, of love, of joy, of All That Is as it is expressed through All That Is.

Know that we, as other expressions of All That Is, are always with you. We love you. We serve you in ways of which you have not dreamed. We are always ready to respond to your cries of pain and anguish as well as shouts of joy, for all are expressions of Divinity experiencing itself always.

We welcome the time wherein the veils of illusion are seen through your perception as simply that, veils which can be readily swept aside with one well-directed movement of deeply desiring to play and rejoice in the Light. That time is now! There is no other 'time,' for eternity exists in a continuum of cycles, events, and evolving life on all levels.

We thank you for this opportunity to communicate with you. Know that we are with you—each and every one of you, always! In love, in Light we come to you. In love, in Light we remain within your hearts. Should any of you have difficulty in your life experiences, please turn to this page and reread this message. It will return you to the Source, the God within yourselves. It is that to which all of you are in the process of awakening.

Blessed Be from One and All to One and All

— *Gehema*

Part II — The Therapy

It is seen that there is most definitely a Light upon the horizon. That Light is one that is composed of the hopes, the dreams, and the prayers of those upon your plane who seek to bring about harmony, peace, and love. That Light is most visible, yet it will take continued efforts on the part of each and every individual, in whatever way they deem necessary or fit.

For those who seek wisdom, let them, through the ray of wisdom, add to that Light and bring forth that Light upon this plane in greater luminescence. For those who seek to be happy, let them look within themselves and see within themselves what it is that truly makes them happy, what makes them feel at home within their hearts, and do what it takes to energize that frequency to live in that. No matter what seems to be going on in your external world, there is a peace, there is a center, a oneness, a unity which transcends your physical plane dimension. And it is this beingness, this Unity, which will carry each and every one of you further and further into the Light.

— Athor, 1989

"We have determined that we do not have sufficient data about the human species and its capacity on the Earth plane. We are unable to gather this data except through a type of direct experience, as we in particular need to understand the processes which humans undergo; how the human consciousness becomes so embroiled and entrapped in the most negative circumstances, thoughts, and feelings. We do not understand the process— how the divinity becomes so obscured. We have a need to understand this process."

— *The Sirius Council of Elders*
Channeled through Athor, August 31, 1991

Chapter 7

A Therapist's Dilemma

And now let us explore how this unusual being discovered that she is not Rose, but Athor. I have used actual transcripts of the therapy sessions that were recorded. These have been only slightly edited to make the material clearer to the reader. A few parts were deleted that did not seem relevant to the therapy. Some of the sentences are not complete, as in normal conversation, and most of these I did not change.

Because of less than adequate recording equipment, I had to rely on my notes for some of the material. Athor wants the reader to know that the memories were often extremely slow in coming through, and there were frequently very long pauses, with much emotion. This is not always evident from the transcripts. Also, the reader will note from the dates on the material that the transcripts are not always in chronological order, since the memories came through only when apparent blocks had been released.

Although the earliest transcripts often did not make much sense to either of us, I felt they should be included to give the reader a better understanding of my initial doubts and utter confusion. At the beginning of the therapy, I could not help but wonder if my client was, indeed, the paranoid-schizophrenic she had been diagnosed as earlier by her college psychiatrist. Was this a case of possession or multiple personality? Why was I investing so much time and energy in a case where there was no monetary gain? Why did I repeatedly risk my professional reputation by giving workshops about this bizarre case at professional conferences?

All of this was going through my mind as I continued to work with Athor, trying to fit together all the pieces of the puzzle in an attempt to make sense out of this experiment. It's clear to me now that there was a soul agreement on my part. Now I understand my role in working with beings like Athor. However, I was totally baffled by all the information coming through Rose-Athor in the beginning, and I often doubted my own sanity.

I have changed Athor's Earth name, exact date of birth, and place of birth, since she wishes to maintain her privacy, but to the best of my knowledge all the other personal data is true. While I cannot prove that any of the information in the transcripts is factual, it all finally seems to fit together. I hope the reader will find this to be an interesting adventure in multidimensional travel. If it stretches your belief system, know that initially I felt the same way. We are all moving into the fifth dimension and I find that my reality continues to shift. I strongly believe that this is necessary for us to survive in these chaotic times on Earth.

Rose, the entity who occupied Athor's body prior to the soul exchange, called me right before Christmas, 1988, to make an appointment. She had seen my picture in an ad in a Sacramento area metaphysical magazine and had the feeling I could help her. Her main problem was Environmental Illness, a life-threatening condition in which a person is highly allergic to almost everything in the environment.

She told me more about her situation, sounding very desperate. Even though I will offer a reduced fee to those who cannot afford my regular fee, Rose did not feel that she could even afford to pay that. From her description of the problem, I was not at all sure that I could help her and felt that, if there were any way to help, this almost certainly would require long-term therapy. I didn't have any experience dealing with a problem such as Environmental Illness and told her I was sorry, but I did not feel there was any way I could take her as a client. I took her telephone number and said I would contact her if I could think of anyone else who might be able to help.

As Christmas drew nearer, I had fewer clients than usual and the conversation with Rose began to bother me. The more I thought about Rose, the more I sensed that I should see her for at least one session. She seemed to feel I was her last chance to get help. I found out later that winter is usually the worst time of the year for her because the mold count is high. Allergy to molds is a particularly severe problem in her case. Rather reluctantly, I called to say I doubted there was any way I could help, but that I was willing to see her for one session to evaluate her case. We scheduled the first appointment for December 22.

During the first session with any client I always take a case history. This usually can be accomplished in a one-hour session. This first session with Rose went on for more three hours. Fortunately, I did not have any other clients after her. I was fascinated with what she told me.

Although the following constitutes a summary of what the reader already has been told about Rose, I am repeating the principal facts in order to give my impressions of her as a client.

Rose was born in Frankfurt, Germany, in 1945. She never knew her father, since he deserted her mother before Rose was born. Many of her earliest memories involve being quite poor. Her mother was often angry with her for reasons Rose did not understand. When Rose was five, her mother married a man who later proved to be psychotic. Shortly after the marriage, the family moved to Canada, where Rose was enrolled in school.

She remembers the children laughing at her because she could not speak English. She made the decision that no one would laugh at her again. Rose learned English rapidly and today exhibits no sign of a foreign accent. She made good grades in school but did not form many bonds with the other students because she always felt quite different from them.

Rose painted a picture of a family that thrived on violence. Although she hated her stepfather on one level, she also felt sorry for him, apparently recognizing from an early age that he was a mentally ill individual. Rose was a reminder to her mother of the man who deserted her when she was in desperate need of financial assistance. She was a reminder to her stepfather of another man formerly involved with the mother. There was little nurturing. Rose felt that she was the caretaker of the family.

When Rose was in her sophomore year in college, she insisted on rooming alone. During that year, Rose had an out-of-body experience that lasted six hours. "I traveled through all the dimensions searching for the 'All That Is.' I had the choice of staying or coming back into the body. I chose to come back because I did not know why I was on Earth to begin with." After this episode, Rose was able to hear people's thoughts word for word.

She had been seeing the college psychiatrist because of the mental abuse she had suffered as a child. Not understanding this "strange" student in any way, the psychiatrist decided that she was paranoid-schizophrenic, which resulted in Rose's confinement to a state mental institution.

After her release from the mental institution, she dropped out of college and began traveling for a period of several years. She finally married a man who had an illness similar to her own (unbeknown to her at the time of the marriage), and they had one daughter. Rose's husband died five years prior to her contacting me. It took many years for Rose's illness to be diagnosed. She was increasingly concerned about her health since she often would be near death when she experienced severe allergy attacks.

I was quite concerned about inducing a trance state with Rose. Even though I did not feel that she was paranoid-schizophrenic, I had never worked with a client before who had been in a mental hospital and been diagnosed as psychotic. If indeed this were a true case of psychosis, it was definitely beyond the scope of an M.F.C.C. However, Rose really did not trust psychiatrists, for obviously good reasons, and despite her bizarre history, she appeared to be quite rational. I knew, however, that most psychiatrists today would very likely come up with a diagnosis of psychosis.

The Diagnostic and Statistical Manual of Mental Disorders (DSM III) defines paranoid-schizophrenia as a type of schizophrenia dominated by persecutory delusions and/or hallucinations with persecutory or grandiose content.

Rose had what could be interpreted as three symptoms: (1) she felt that she had been misunderstood most of her life because she was so different from other people and thus, in a sense, felt that she had been persecuted but had good reason for feeling this way, according to her story; (2) she had what could be termed grandiose delusions because she felt that she had unusual abilities not possessed by other people; and (3) throughout her life she had had numerous psychic experiences which could be interpreted as hallucinations.

I also found Rose to be extremely suspicious of me, even though she had wanted very much to come to me for therapy. She seemed to be testing me during the entire first session. It really did not surprise me that a psychiatrist had diagnosed her as paranoid-schizophrenic.

A number of my clients had been psychic, but none to the extent claimed by Rose. I felt it advisable only to proceed with therapy on the condition that Rose sign an agreement releasing me from liability, just in case severe problems developed as the result of the hypnotherapy sessions. I also made it clear to Rose that, since she was not able to pay me, this would be considered research. I have never had any negative results from my work with clients, but this was strictly experimental. I was not at all sure that I could help her and there were some risks involved, but I seem to thrive on challenging cases.

Chapter 8

First Session: Channeling or Possession?

W hen Rose arrived for her second session on December 27, she seemed much more relaxed. Apparently I had passed her test, despite all my stated concerns about proceeding with therapy. I directed her to get her body as comfortable as possible on my contour chair but before we started, she needed to get some fresh air. She went over to the atrium door and opened it. As time went on, this became standard procedure every time she came to my office. Rose said that she got claustrophobia in places that did not have fresh air. This posed a problem in the wintertime, from my point of view, but I learned to accept it. Later we found out that she had suffocated in a past life. She also requested a cloth to put over her eyes to shut out as much light as possible.

I induced Rose into a hypnotic state and began our first session. The reader will note that I have included the conversation after the hypnotic session because I decided to leave the tape recorder on. This conversation gives the flavor of the therapy when Rose was not in a trance state. Notice that the language is quite different.

First Hypnosis Session, December 27, 1988

E: Evelyn
R: Rose
E: We want to go back to the very beginning—what caused Rose's physical problems? Going back to the source of these problems in Rose's life, let me know what comes to mind. One, two, three. What is happening?

R: It was a choice that was made eons and eons ago in which this being did choose to come to the Earth with the sole intent and purpose of helping those on this plane who did not see the Light. In the course of the many sojourns upon this plane and this planet you call Earth, she became trapped, as it were, feeling much sorrow and compassion for those who seemed to exhibit a lesser Light, though in truth were but asleep.

In the past ten to fifteen lifetimes, this one has chosen to take upon the bodies with which this being has incarnated in those cycles, the ills, the misfortunes, the trials, the tribulations of all those who came upon her. This lifetime is the culmination of that repayment, as it were, wherein she took upon herself that which in truth she should have let go, but, understanding not, she chose to carry it upon herself.

E: Since she has chosen this, at this point in her life, can she make a different choice and choose no longer to carry this burden?

R: Yes. If she is willing to release her hold upon this world.

E: What would that involve? How can she release her hold upon this world?

R: She must sanctify the moment and be but in grace.

E: Can you explain to Rose more about how she goes about sanctifying? She needs to understand what that means.

R: When the realization bonds the past, the present, and the future, it is but one moment ever present in the Infinite One. The comprehension will be there of sanctifying the moment and living in the grace of the Oneness of All. (This made no sense to me.)

E: Will this release her from her physical problems, as well as the other problems she has?

R: The physical is but a mere reflection of the illusion of that which you call time. In truth, it has no existence.

E: I want to clarify my own thinking to be sure I understand. You said that she voluntarily took on all these problems of the people from all these past lives, and brought all of this into this incarnation. Am I correct in interpreting at least that part?

R: That is correct.

E: What did Rose hope to achieve in doing that? She must have had some purpose in doing that to begin with.

R: As was said, she chose to come to this plane to help those here who seem to exhibit a lesser Light. In truth they were but merely asleep, and in so doing she became trapped, as it were, for she believed that in order to help she must take into her personalized physical form that which was not yet physicalized in others. She hoped to spare them the physicalization of their misjudgments or their misunderstandings which would cause them in their physical illusions much pain—much suffering. Though, in truth, that also is merely an illusion. Yet those upon this plane cannot see it as such.

E: You have explained to Rose what is necessary for her to make a different decision at this point. If she is able to sanctify herself and live in grace, what path should she take for the rest of this particular lifetime— what path would enable her to accomplish what she feels at this point in life is important for her to accomplish in this lifetime?

R: There is but one motion, the motion of life and evolution of expanding awareness—expanding consciousness, as it were. We do not look upon her as having a particular path, for that is the path of life, and there are "many myriad ways..." of experiencing life. This is but one extension of the greater whole from whence she came. Do not trouble yourselves with petty thoughts of life's purposes and life's paths for they, in truth, have but little meaning to the whole of That Which Is.

Many of you have been told that all is as it should be, that in truth it is so. You and she and others wish to analyze, to compartmentalize. Such is but the attempt of the limited mind to comprehend that which is incomprehensible, making finite that which has no beginning and no end.

E: We ask for your help because we don't understand everything that is going on here on planet Earth, and we need your help. Is there anything else that you can tell Rose and me that will help give enlightenment to this situation—to help us understand better?

R: She is on the path, as it were. Those are terms with which you and others are familiar.

E: Yes, we understand that.

R: And in that path, she will soon see that all is one and one is all, and that there is no need to take on what would seem to be another's. For the illusion, thus generated, can only be recognized and accepted and possessed by the mind that deals in illusion. When the recognition occurs, as it were, the illusion will disappear. The sickness, as it were, will be no more. The pains, the suffering, the earthly...will be no more. There will only be All That Is, in the Oneness of All.

E: Am I speaking to one of the Masters? Would you be willing to identify yourself?

R: You, my child, are speaking to the "All That Is," once and forevermore will be, of which you are an undeniable, indescribable spark, together with all other sparks which come to make the "All That Is."

E: Is Rose very often in touch with the entity that I am talking to? What is her connection with you? Is it any different from mine?

(I was extremely confused since I had never heard the terminology, "All That Is," before.)

R: Yes. It is a matter of interpretation—how one's concepts filter through the various vibrational frequencies which you term the mind. In her case, the frequencies are often assumed to be a higher being who has come periodically to save her from the pitfalls and snares of human follies. She has been shown many times the choices which were available, and was most conscious of those choices she didst make. In Earth terms, she would be considered the elder child.

E: Will there be more Earth lives for Rose?

R: Perhaps, but only if she so chooses.

E: I guess it's her choice at this point.

R: Yes. If she wishes to tie herself to this thread of illusion so she may once again return, then that will be so. Otherwise, no.

E: Thank you. You have given us both great insights.

R: Are there things you wish to ask?

E: Yes. I would like to ask a question just for myself about one of my clients, a boy who was killed and made his transition in an accident about a month ago. He seems to have had repeated Earth lives where he was killed violently in some way at a young age. When does the turning point come for a soul like this—when can there be a different choice? Each life has been very traumatic for him. This time he was twelve years old. His name is Benjamin Sparks.

R: What matters not is the repetition or the numbers, as you call it, of so-called lifetimes. It matters not if it is five thousand. The numbers matter not. What matters is the degree of, as you would say, receptivity, the degree of awareness when the spark is recognized as a growing flame within the being in and of itself. Once this has been recognized, the further steps taken to realize the flame as being all and yet in one.

This boy you speak of has not yet reached the awareness of the individualized flame within his heart. The spirit of this entity has tried repeatedly to assert itself—to reveal itself, yet the mind frequencies of the repeated incarnations of this being have sufficiently obstructed that realization—that feeling. It is as if the entity does not believe it has any self-worth. Thus it repeatedly punishes itself in a very limited fashion here on this plane by taking form and thus then destroying the form for no apparent purpose except to relive its illusion of worthlessness.

E: Thank you. It's a possibility that he may have had that spark towards the very end because he came to me for help after his transition. With the help of a psychic client, I assisted Ben in going to the Light. One more question. Would Rose be able to go into a trance herself—self-induced—and have you come through her again in order to have other people ask questions that could give them greater enlightenment? Is that possible? Are you willing to do this?

R: This entity has no wants or desires or wishes to the contrary. However, this being needs some guidance—a pat on the arm or holding her hand a little bit. Something to that effect, for she does not feel she can truly access that which is as yet.

E: Very good. I give you a great deal of thanks for coming through today. I tell you now, for the time being, farewell, so I can directly address Rose and have her come back into her body here in this room.

Rose, you have been given the privilege of having this entity come through you—a very highly spiritual entity—to give both you and me information. Because you have been the vehicle for this, this can be viewed at a deep level as a healing, as a way for you to do as directed to live in grace. You basically know how to do this, I'm sure. I feel that this entity, this spiritual being, can be contacted again by you—perhaps not speaking through you the way the entity did today, but having him give you spiritual guidance within your own mind, so this is probably a teacher or guide, some particular help for you especially, so be sure to call for help when you need it.

Feel confident in yourself that being the bodily vehicle for this to come through is a healing experience. (I continued to give instruction to the subconscious mind for healing the body.)

And now, when I count to five, slowly come back into the body, feeling completely regenerated, in mind, body, and spirit, and feeling very, very wonderful. One, two, three, four, five. Slowly open your eyes when you are ready.

E: Well, it will be an interesting experience to listen to this again. Do you have any reflections on it? (The trance session had ended, and we continue talking in a fully conscious state. I had left the tape recorder on.)

R: My mind is always like this. Every time I get anything that comes through me, it's like, "So what." I've heard stuff like this before. Similar things have come through before.

E: That's totally understandable. How has this come through before?

R: I've done readings and things, and I used to work with a friend of mine. In fact, six months before my husband died, I don't know how it happened, I wasn't doing it deliberately. He was sitting on my bed and all of a sudden I went into a trance I'd never been in before. This thing kept saying it was the Father and how my husband was trying to kill me and what was he doing to me, and my husband was completely transformed.

In all the years he lived with me I had never seen him react like that. He was terrified of death and things like that. He actually knelt down and started crying, and my body was going through all kinds of weird stuff. It was really like giving physical birth. It hurt a lot. Energy was taken out of my own life force in the form of a spirit. He was told that the spirit would be with him until he reached enlightenment, wherever he went, wherever he was.

All of a sudden we had a very deep exchange, and he was prepared—he accepted the fact that he was ready to go from the Earth plane. Six months later he physically died. I was preparing him, too, on the conscious level, because my friend and I had been trying to get some spirits to answer a few questions when all of a sudden Shiva came, unannounced, and just said, very quickly, "George is going to die in six months." I took that and put it on the shelf. Let's get on with it and back to other stuff that was totally unrelated, and sure enough, six months later he left the plane. After he died, the next day it was awful for me.

Rose then related her story of being told that she had saved her husband two hundred incarnations.

E: That sounds like a very difficult marriage.

R: Yes, it was.

E: You obviously have the ability to channel.

R: Oh, yes.

E: Also, you sound as if you are somewhat afraid of it.

R: Yes, because I have also had severe allergies. And I have always danced on a very thin line. I've heard other voices as well. I've had experiences where it felt like what you humans term hell. It was very strange because I went down; usually I experienced going up and out. This one time, years ago, I went down, down, down. I thought I had better check it out and see what all this is about. There was this huge hand, I remember, and I was like a bar of soap. It kept trying to grab me and I kept slipping out. It couldn't hold onto me. People hand me their garbage. Sometimes I'm not very conscious that it's their garbage and not mine. I'm like a sponge, and it comes in and pretty soon it's like, oh, I feel this and I feel that, and sometimes I'm too sick to really question why.

E: Psychic people have a real problem with that. They pick up all those vibrations.

R: So, I'm really, really leery of the information I receive. Past-life readings for other people is no big deal. To me, it's all very boring. I've done it for over twenty years.

E: It's not what you want to do with your life, then?

R: I've never charged, and I've never made money. I've suffered and had economic problems, and I just don't know. I guess it's such a repetition of what I've done in past lives, and for me I guess I don't see any growth in that.

Then I had a memorable lifetime where it took a good five years before the answer came to that. I always had this mortal fear of making a mistake. My friend I had been working with in Sacramento said, "What do you fear the most?" I said, "Making a mistake." She thought I meant on this level. I said, "No, I make mistakes all the time." That's not what I'm talking about. It's a cosmic mistake. Because I had a lifetime where I saw I was sitting on a mountain top and I decided, I guess, I can go. I just rose up and left. Left the body sitting there in meditation and I took off. This was the thing that drew me back, and this explained why in this lifetime I was born to my mother.

I could never figure that out for years, either. Because it seemed to be almost accidental, in a sense. I always felt that I was forced into her womb and in actuality I finally realized why. It happened because in that lifetime I had promised my disciples that I would not leave the body until they were all spiritually ready. When I left, I left because it was my decision to go. I did not take into account my word to them and my promise. It was just like I decided I'd go. I left with a tremendous guilt and a sense of responsibility.

Because of that guilt and that responsibility, in this life, I had already picked out my mother in a church in Europe. She would have been ideal for my wishes. All of a sudden, the woman was killed in a car accident about three or four months into the pregnancy and I was catapulted out. And just as quickly as the soul went out, it was immediately sucked back down into my present mother's womb and I remember just feeling that God had deserted and abandoned me and the gods were out to get me because I had her for a mother. Even going into the womb, I had to go through cancer cells. Yuck! She had cancer at thirty-three and had a complete hysterectomy. I was born when she was twenty-one, so technically it was in the aura all that time, for twelve years.

My half-sister called me before Christmas and said, "Oh, you sound just like you did when we were living together. You were always so positive." Then I remembered, as a matter of fact, yes, I was the one who held the family up. They were unwittingly dealing with Black Magic without knowing it, essentially.

When I left, they had poltergeists in the house and all this uncontrollable energy that I would not allow in when I was there. My mother almost had a nervous breakdown when I left. It was like, "Get out, get out, you're causing all of these problems." About a week before, I had told them I was leaving and said, "I'm not the cause of your problems. You'll find out." It's been the pattern. I've had people attack me—try to kill me physically in this life. Later on, through the years, because they would project all that on me, and I had been helping them. I always said I went where angels feared to tread. Every single time it turned out that's right. Something happened. I mean, I've stared death in the face.

E: It certainly sounds like it from everything you've told me. We need to stop.

I was so entranced by this that I temporarily forgot I was supposed to be doing therapy. I'd had only one other client who had started channeling when hypnotized, a young man so frightened by the celestial messages coming through him that he never returned for another appointment.

I was taken aback by Rose's comments that she had done this before. She felt that it was nonproductive and boring. This was "old hat" to her. As I listened to her comments, I began to feel that she was just humoring me by going along with my instructions to heal the cells. During the hypnotic session, I was thinking that this was an unusual experience for Rose. An entity was speaking through her, surfacing with the intent of helping Rose's healing. What simplistic thinking! As she told me, this was nothing new to her, but it certainly was new for me.

In trying to analyze this session, considering all the information we now have, I theorize in hindsight that the entity was talking about the former occupant, Rose, taking on the karma of all those she had associated with in past lives.

We have recently clarified that the soul who left the body on the mountain was also Rose. She apparently "ascended." Therefore, Rose must have been a highly evolved entity herself, thus earning the right to end her incarnations here on Earth in this cycle. However, because she felt she had made a mistake at a soul level in ascending, the soul decided to incarnate once again to balance this karma. Thus began a series of difficult life cycles.

On the other hand, the entity is talking about Athor in stating, "This being did choose to come to Earth with the sole intent and purpose of helping those on this plane who did not see the Light." Of course, we also have learned that Athor has more specific purposes, but assisting humanity is still the general mission of all of the so-called "Light Workers" incarnated at this time on planet Earth.

With regard to future incarnations, this is also the choice of the Athor soul, since the Rose soul apparently will not return to Earth. At the time of this first session, I was confused by the entity identifying itself as the "All That Is." This is the terminology we now use for God. I theorize that Athor was actually speaking, but Rose's conscious mind was filtering the information enough to make some sense to her, even though it made little sense to me.

I believe that this was probably Athor speaking in this session, but, of course, we did not know that then. She was quite familiar with the "All That Is," thus, the identification with God, since Athor had not yet surfaced from her subconscious mind.

Chapter 9

Enter Athor: The Mystery Deepens

Our next appointment was on January 2, 1989. Rose felt that she could trust me; she had much more that she wanted to tell me. She related her many experiences with the kundalini. Since Athor discusses this (see last chapter), I will not go into the details. She was finally satisfied that this had been accomplished in a positive fashion. Since very few of us are ever able to reach this point of evolvement, I felt that perhaps the raising of the kundalini was one of the explanations for Rose's unusual abilities. On the other hand, she had many remarkable experiences long before she'd had her final kundalini experience.

Rose expressed a strong, long-standing desire to leave the Earth. She had never considered herself suicidal, but her physical problems were so overwhelming that at this point in therapy she was tired of fighting them. She was ready to give up. She had never felt as if the Earth were home, and she wanted desperately to "go home" again.

We discussed her channeling ability further. She said she would feel much more comfortable about the information if she could just step aside and let another entity take over. She felt as if her own personality judged some of the information. Such astounding and sometimes quite upsetting information came through about people that she did not want to be responsible for the information. At her suggestion, I agreed to lead her through a tunnel into the Light prior to asking any questions. She felt as if she could rest in the Light if her mind were asleep.

We also discussed the possibility that this spirit being channeled by Rose constituted a form of possession. Maybe this channeled being was creating the physical problems experienced by Rose.

I decided that the therapy would be led by Rose, not me. She had an extremely strong personality, and I sensed that traditional approaches simply would not work with her. We scheduled her next appointment for one week later.

Second Hypnosis Session, January 9, 1989

E: If there is some other entity in Rose's body besides the soul essence that is Rose, let that entity come forth. I would like to speak to that entity.

Give this energy a form. Let it be known. Who else is there besides Rose?

R: This being has the capacity to allow others to come through the energy field into Earth frequencies at such times as she so desires. Oftentimes this may be mistaken by those who cannot see the entire auric field as a possession of the physical body, and in truth it is but an opening in the outer layers of the auric field or in the contact and the connections made. The soul residing within this physical vehicle is but one individual essence.

E: Identify yourself. Who am I talking to now?

R: I am that which is and was and forever more.

E: Am I again contacting the same spirit energy that I talked to before when Rose was here?

R: Yes.

E: Very good. Thank you for identifying yourself. Is it all right for Rose to completely leave her body at this point? Is it all right to have you lead her through the tunnel and into the infinite Light for her to get a rest? What is best for her?

R: What she perceives as a need for rest is but the need of this entity's mind frequencies to be shut down, as it were, so they are no longer accessible to any and all outside influences that may wish to knock on the door to seek entry and seek to be heard and seek to speak. She has as yet not mastered the art of closing that door whenever one does knock. Thus she has misunderstood and feels that it is necessary for the soul to leave. For in truth, it has never been here in time and space but resides, as it were, in the All, and manifests but a small part of itself through this physical vehicle.

E: I would like to ask you to speak in terms that are understandable to Earth beings such as myself and Rose. What can you tell Rose about her wish to go home? What can she do for herself to help her feel better about being here on Earth?

R: She must concentrate and focus on the beam of Light emanating from the Third Eye, extending outward into space to the Infinite Source. If she allows her mind to travel along this beam of Light, she will come to understand that which she now misinterprets. She will come to see that her fears are the darkness that she now perceives to be so real.

E: What is the best method that will allow you to come through Rose and talk to me or to anyone else who desires to talk to you?

R: The method you have selected is sufficient.

E: Very good, thank you. What else can you tell Rose that she can do and is supposed to do to help her emotionally handle her problems? You have already given some insight into this. Is there anything else you can add to it?

R: The human state of mind consistently seeks to find new and different answers to very simple inalienable truths, laws as it were, of universal existence. There are not ten million different answers. There are very few variations on the main theme, and again it is stated that if the mind can concentrate on the beam of Light and enter it, flow with it to its source, then that which is termed emotional problems will also cease to be.

E: Is this beam of Light a particular color, or is it a white Light?

R: It is white, but not a white as you perceive.

E: Will Rose recognize this Light when she is able to focus in and concentrate on that beam?

R: Yes, but it is seen that it is a process that will not occur overnight. as this being has many fears, and once she does contact through the mind this beam, this Light, she will no longer hold back and shut down and thus not allow the truth to penetrate.

E: If Rose were to follow this beam of Light completely, be absorbed in this beam of Light that you are speaking of, would she be able to come back into this body and be perfectly safe in this body?

R: The body you speak of, and which she now recognizes, is but of an illusionary vehicle. As such, to return to that body is not possible. However, the body, so called, to which she will return will outwardly manifest as this present vehicle. However, in essence it will be transformed.

E: (I interpreted this as meaning that everything on Earth is, in some sense, an illusion.) Will it be transformed into a healthy body, free of the physical problems that she has been experiencing?

R: In the body composed of Light, there can be no physical disease.

E: When Rose returns to this body, will she be able to function still as an Earth being, since her body will be a body of Light?

R: When she chooses to manifest in a form which would appear to be much denser, yes, she would.

E: From what realm is your main home? Can you tell me a little bit more about the realm you are from?

R: We are from that which is termed Amoria, plane of the Gods, which in vibratory lingo is the Angelic Kingdom.

E: All right, the Angelic Kingdom. (This was such amazing information to me that I didn't know what other questions to ask, so I changed the subject.) I would like to ask you to examine, from your perspective, Evelyn's body and her ankle, her left ankle and foot. Can you give some information on what is going on with that ankle and foot that will help her?

R: It is seen that there is an obstruction in the third and fourth cervical vertebrae, thus creating a blockage. This obstruction further influences and affects the venous circulation in the lower left leg. Another further complication is the twist in the ankle of the left leg. There are three major clots, which are energy blockages, but also have translated into the circulatory system. It is seen that if she were to get proper acupuncture with a qualified individual, this area would clear up.

However, the back—there seems to be two bones—I hear, calcification, two to three vertebrae, and the discs are almost non-existent. This would take intensive work in many different areas over a period of time, as it were, between chiropractic and the entity's own visualization of restructuring that spinal column, those vertebrae, stretching and rebuilding them. It is possible to do this. But it will require much mind power in order to effect the necessary changes.

E: Thank you. Before I say good-bye to you today, do you have any other message for Rose or for me?

R: Yes. It is imperative for you, in your meditations, to generate energy in the thymus area as energy radiating outward from this area here (pointing to the heart), outward, golden Light. As it is seen, there is an obstruction occurring in here. And you can prevent any circulatory disturbances which will affect the arms and shoulders and will create pain. Release through that Light all obstructions from this area.

E: I understand. Is there anything more for Rose?

R: Yes. She should remember that if she calls upon her soul essence, she calls upon the All, she will always receive her answer, though she may not comprehend and it may not appear in the manner in which she had expected. She has been given information to travel into the infinite Light. Yet, in her frame of mind and understanding, she presumed that this would mean that another being would necessarily come and occupy the space, as it were.

She would wish to skip a step, and that is not possible. She does not wish to hear that which seems to imply that she must work, because when she begins to follow the beam of Light, the resistance will become greatly magnified and all sorts of sundry fears, terrors, and destructive emotions may surface. She is but purging that which she has taken on through the centuries and so densified and physicalized that it would seem to have taken on a reality of its own. This she must remember when she utilizes the Light and meditation.

I once again found myself caught up in the channeling experience. Little of what was said made sense to me. In listening to the tapes of our sessions, in retrospect, I believe that I entered into a trance state myself during these sessions. I really had not intended to ask any questions about myself but because I did, I discovered Rose's ability to scan the body. Strangely enough, I was not surprised at this point that she was able to do this. Although Athor is able to scan the body for physical problems, she is not willing to do this any longer without the person receiving the reading signing a medical disclaimer. She is slowly learning the "system" under which we must operate on Earth.

While all of this was quite fascinating, I did not feel that we were getting anywhere in terms of therapy. I have not been able to locate the tape recording of our next session on January 16 but according to my notes, a different entity identified itself as Athor:

"I was pre-mortal in times before civilized consciousness, a time of great darkness, great density, the beginning of evolution. I did not wish to be here. It was dark. Where am I? I do not know where I am. I cannot see or hear."

Then Rose suddenly found herself back in the womb. There was much emotion as she went through the trauma of the birth experience.

After this session, we still did not understand what was going on. Several weeks elapsed because of my busy schedule. During that time, Rose asked a friend to assist her in going into a trance state. Both Rose and I were beginning to wonder if this "Athor" were possessing her body. This channeling, unlike the earlier one identifying "Athor," triggered the spontaneous birth experience. During this experience, Rose's body curled up in the fetal position. She cried and expressed much fear and disgust. We later found that this was the birth of Rose, not Athor, although Athor had been talking immediately prior to the experience.

I have no explanation for this except that it would seem now that the Athor soul had been assisting in the therapy process all along, although information came through in bits and pieces. However, both Rose and I were still wondering about "spirit possession" at this point.

Rose asked for the assistance of a friend to continue working on the release of the Athor spirit. When Rose returned for the next session, she felt that Athor had gone. But she was wrong.

"What is difficult for this vehicle and the cellular memory to encompass is the fact that the consciousness is indeed called "Extraterrestrial." However, the body physically is not. Thus, there is a great discrepancy, as the physical memory banks of the physical vehicle are such that, until they are purified and released, the final stage of the energy transference cannot be accomplished and completed.

So we have here, in essence, a duality of consciousness. For, you see, the physical body has a consciousness of its own cellular memory and genetic makeup which is indeed vivified by the consciousness from the Sirius Group. However, we have been attempting to make the full transition and transmission and have not as yet succeeded due to the impurities which yet reside within the cellular mechanism of this third-density vehicle. This includes impurities in all major organs and cellular makeup which also includes the brain, the physical brain."

— *Athor, December 1989*

Chapter 10

Rose Meets Extraterrestrials: the Doubts Begin

E ven though Rose felt that Athor had gone, I thought we needed to go back to the little girl, Rose, to get more information in order to find out what this business regarding Athor was all about. The session on February 6, 1989, was finally a big breakthrough to clarify Rose's situation. Immediately prior to this session, Rose told me she had the feeling that something had happened to her when she was three years and two months old.

Hypnosis Session, February 6, 1989

E: Go back to when you became emotionally upset. We're going to go back to that little girl, to that little girl who is now three years, two months old. She has had many painful experiences already for one so young and she is much more grown-up than most girls might be at that age. We want to go back and meet her again. It is time to remember. While this is coming through, Rose, I ask for the loving protection of your Guardian Spirits, not the beings that are from other realms, but the beings that were taking care of Rose when she was this little girl. I call on those particular spirits that were hovering around her, noticing what was happening to her, taking care of her, and I also call on mine to help with this process. One, two, three. Tell me what is happening. You are a little girl.

R: Driving in the countryside. It's a nice sunny day. And I'm really happy because I like being in the car. I've never been in a car. We passed lots of houses. There's a church there on the left. Maybe it's Sunday—there's people around. There's a very sharp turn in the road ... and they drive on.

E: Who is in the car with you?

R: I guess they're my relatives. They look like they're all men. They look like men. They don't look like people. They wear white robes.

E: Have you seen them before?

R: Yes. When I was six or seven months old. It was very dark and alone, and I was hungry, and I was crying, and nobody came. (Rose begins crying.) It hurts, it hurts!

E: Stay with the emotion, that's fine, but I want you to continue.

R: They fed me. One stood on one side of me and one on the other side, when I was six or seven months old. They put some kind of tube in...it doesn't look to be real...green liquid...didn't touch me but they felt like they had. But they fed me.

E: And while this was happening, Rose, what were your feelings? Were you feeling as if you were grateful to them? Were you afraid in any way? Did you feel they were being good to you?

R: Surprised.

E: Surprised? That it was okay, because they were taking care of you?

R: I had to understand that they were my mother and father.

E: How was this message given to you?

R: Because they told me.

E: Did they talk at all?

R: Out loud?

E: Did you ever sense they were giving you messages through their minds? (Athor nods "yes.") Is there anything else you want to say before you move back to the car?

R: Feels strange. They were so quiet. Not like the people I know around me. (Rose is speaking of her Earth parents.) Those people were very noisy inside. They brought darkness where they walked They would make a bright room dark. These two make a dark room bright. I couldn't understand, but I felt safe. I didn't know where I was. Why was I with those people? (Rose again is referring to her mother and stepfather.) And why were those two (the extraterrestrials) there? Why should I have to be with those people? It's so confusing.

E: When you say those other people, are you speaking of your Earth parents? (Athor nods "yes." At the time, I was not clear about this.)

I want you to move ahead in time now to your next meeting with these beings, or beings like them, and it may have been the car, or it might have been even before that. I'm going to count backwards from five to one until you get that memory back again. The very next time you have a meeting with these beings or others like them, five, remember you are still Rose, you're still talking from Rose's viewpoint—four, three, two, one, getting in touch with these beings.

R: Some kind of a sandbox. I was making figures and designs.

E: Can you tell me about the picture?

R: It's like there's (motioned with her hands to indicate a symbol) on top of—like there's two lines underneath.

E: So it's sort of like a symbolic-type thing that you were looking at? But you don't understand it right now?Did they give you any message about this figure?

R: It's a symbol of the universe, the two beings are saying. From the outer-most to the innermost infinitesimal atom. "It is there." the beings say, pointing to the sky. "It is here," as he makes a circle around us all. "And it is here," he said, pounding his staff into the Earth.

E: These are all messages they are giving to you telepathically. Is that correct?

R: Yes.

E: How old are you?

R: Two.

E: That's a great deal of knowledge for a two-year-old to try to make any sense out of. Now, when this happened, what were the feelings of you, Rose, two-year-old Rose. What were the feelings at that point?

R: I don't understand.

E: Were you at all frightened?

R: No.

E: Were these the same two beings that came to you when you were a baby?

R: Yes.

E: Is there anything else you want to say about that experience before we move on and go to your next meeting?

R: Something like those key rings, those rings that snap together. This was a gold ring, a key ring that snaps, it wasn't just one. I could hold it in my hand. It had many sides, and they let me play with it. It was like a gyroscope.

E: Is this similar to the helix symbol that you told me about when you first came in today?

R: It's similar, but it's not the same thing. This is a key given—at this stage.

E: I see, it's kind of a progressive stage, then. Did they then take that with them when they left? They let you play with it, let you experience it. (Athor nods "yes") All right, good. Let's move on ahead to the next meeting with the beings.

R: My mother—the woman who says she's my mother—bought me a bal-loon—the woman who says she's my mother.

E: Your Earth mother?

R: Yes. She bought me a balloon, colors painted on it. I let it go. It was an accident, and it went way, way, way up in the sky, and I got very sad because I lost the balloon, and I couldn't go way, way up in the sky. Like that golden thing they had—I wanted to do that. I was crying and she came, the one who said she was my mother. She was angry that I lost the balloon because she didn't have much money. And they're pointing to the balloon. And they're asking me, do you want to go? Yeah, sure. I don't like it here. They're telling me I can fly like that. They say they'll be back, and we will take you up into the sky.

E: How old are you now?

R: Two years, nine months.

E: Is there anything else you want to add to that before we move ahead in time?

R: No.

E: I want Rose, the little girl, to move on to the next encounter with these beings.

R: I'm lying in bed. I don't feel good. I don't want to be here. Everything is dead. Nobody understands me. They can't talk like we do. They say words that don't mean anything. They don't say what they mean, and I don't understand who these people are.

E: Are these people you're speaking of your Earth parents?

R: All of the people. I feel like I'm dying. My skin is crawling.

E: Get into the feeling.

R: Something is coming out of my skin. All over. I don't understand. It's so dead in there. Something is coming out of my body. And they take it.

E: Is somebody else there? Are the beings there?

R: Yes. It's very different from them. You can see through it. It's shaped like me, but you can see through it. I see a cord going from in here (points to her solar plexus) to the head of this other me, and they're taking the other me some place.

E: The other you that was Rose? Do you have a sense that the one they're taking is what used to be Rose?

R: Yes.

E: How old are you now?

R: Three years and two months.

E: (There was a long pause while the realization that this really must be a Soul Exchange entered my consciousness.) Before we go any further, concentrate right now on looking at that shell that was Rose and send your total love and gratitude to this little girl who was willing to give up her body to let the new being that is now you use her body. Connect with that little girl. And, again, let her know that her Earth parents may not have been able to love her but you love her with a tremendous amount of love and you send her gratitude and Light. Know that very soon she will be aware of being able to float as she wants to, to fly, to be Light and not darkness. Feel the happiness of that little girl who is now able to do what she really wanted to do.

R: It was not a little girl.

E: Tell me what you mean by that.

R: It was a being from another constellation.

E: Are you speaking of this baby from the time you've described her?

R: Yes.

E: Was it a little girl in an Earth body?

R: In an Earth body.

E: But she was not like a regular little girl at all. Okay, now tell me, what was she, then?

R: This was a being who was trapped in the interstellar magnetic force field. Somehow accidentally.

E: I see. (Actually, I was totally puzzled.)

R: And the being came from Alpha Centauri. It is the one who did not wish to be here, and knew nothing of whence it came or why it came.

(There is a lengthy explanation of the being from Alpha Centauri in Chapter 16. This being entered the Rose body prior to this incarnation, when the body was being experimented on by extraterrestrials.)

E: Explain a little bit more about Alpha Centauri. Is this another galaxy? Can you explain that further so I can understand it?

R: It is a star cluster.

E: I'd like to ask a lot of questions, but our main purpose this morning is to go through this experience to let this particular body who still calls herself Rose have a better understanding. So let's go back. The being has left the body, the being that really was not supposed to be here. Let's find out more about the being that now has this body that used to be called Rose. Who is now in the body to make it be a living being as we think of it down here on Earth? Get back in that three-year, two-month-old body—the first sensations.

R: Sadness.

E: Sadness, yes. I don't think we necessarily want to get the sadness again. Let's just take a few more breaths. You know everything that has happened in this lifetime. No matter who the being might be in the body, that information is still in the subconscious mind but in order to interpret some of this information, we may need to have some of the teachers and some of the beings from other realms interpret. But again, I want this coming from the physical body as much as possible. You are in a body here on Earth and whatever the reason for this is, you, as a body on Earth, need to understand this.

Let's go back to that point where you see this cord coming—I want a little clarification on that. The way I understood it, there was a cord going from the area you pointed to at the solar plexus, and it was going to the head of the other being. Now the clarification I would like to get on this is just for scientific interest.

R: These beings normally attach from the Third Eye into any forms with which they come in contact.

E: With this new body, again, get back to being three years, two months old, and let's take it again from there. What do you wish to be called?

R: Whom are you addressing?

E: I am addressing the entity that is now in Rose's body. Rose, as we know her, has left. That is my understanding. And she really was not supposed to be here to begin with. This particular entity that is now in Rose's body. I ask two questions: first, what shall I call you?

R: I am Athor.

E: My second question: why have you, Athor, made this exchange? You knew it was going to be very difficult for you because you're aware, I'm sure, of the problems of being in an Earth body. Why were you willing to make this exchange?

R: It has been seen that the planetary currents upon the face of this Earth are such that a transference of intergalactic magnitude must be affected for the continuation of this species upon this planet.

E: Is it your mission, then, to help with this?

R: Yes.

E: We already know, to some extent, many things that have happened to you, Athor. Is there anything from the time when you entered her body coming forward to the present time that you feel I particularly need to know, or that you need to bring to the conscious mind of this body? Because, as Athor, there are many, many things that you must know in the subconscious mind that need to be brought to consciousness at this point.

R: We have already said that it will take from one to two of your Earth years for the complete assimilation of the data that is necessary from all these different aspects, as it were. The human frequency is extremely limited. We must raise the vibrational levels of all those we come in contact with in order to affect the proper intergalactic transmission, as it were.

You, upon this plane, have some knowledge, have an inkling, of what is to be in terms of energy transference and exchange, yet you do not know and do not have the complete picture yet. Within the next fifteen to twenty-five years you will have access to this information. There will be many of you upon the face of the Earth who will not be ready for such transformation. It is seen that those beings will go elsewhere.

You have, at this time, upon the face of this Earth, much upheaval. The vibrational frequencies are in an uproar, as is always the case when there are cataclysmic changes occurring on all multi-levels of the universal scheme and dimension. As within, so without. You upon this plane are not yet awake to the effect you have upon all other life forms in this galaxy.

Thus it is that we, those of us who do perceive these effects, have taken an interest and must, of necessity, be of assistance for the further evolution, the culmination of the grand plan as it were. That which you perceive as the Father, the Son, and the Holy Spirit is what we speak of as the Grand Triune.

E: Athor, that is information that is similar to what you said before but you're giving some different aspects of it, so I thank you. It is very important, since you are functioning in an Earth body, to know what should be your particular role in helping to bring forth this higher vibration here on Earth.

Rose, as I have known her, exhibits a number of talents. Healing is one of them she would like to develop further. Channeling, as she is, and having you speak, is another avenue and she clearly seems to be functioning on two different levels—as you and as her own self—because she had to make this other self a reality for a long time. Please clarify further. I am still confused.

R: The Rose you perceive is but the sum total of the memories of the being which heretofore is no longer residing within this physical body.

E: Yes, I'm beginning to understand that. Give me some information, Athor, so I can help work with you to develop whatever it is that is your main mission because, as I stated, there are several talents. What is the one or several talents that need to be further developed and mastered in this body?

R: It is seen that as the aspects reveal themselves, the guidance, as you term it, is forthcoming through the avenues of books, lectures, articles, and from the channelings within. If you would wish to direct the earthly aspect of this being, to bring it into a closer harmony, as it were, with that which now speaks, then you may be of great assistance, for you have the inner knowingness from past lives of what is the so-called missing link between several of your substrata upon this planet Earth.

There have been many, many life forms upon this planet Earth since the time of its conception.

You have within yourself the memories of those times. The memories of those struggles, memories of those joys, pleasures, and so forth. Call upon that which is in you, which is of the highest essence, and you will be guided to ground this being, as it were, more fully into your present Earth lineage. Call upon the inner knowledge of healing which lies within you. Bring that forth through guidance for this vehicle. In that manner, you can provide a most beneficial service to this being here. For you, if you wish, will be guided to tap those reservoirs within yourself. You have knowledge which this one does not, due to the nature of your experiences, and this knowledge is valuable and beneficial to not only this being but many others. This is the inner bond that has allowed this opening to occur in present Earth time here.

E: Thank you. That gives me a great deal to think about. (I asked myself: "Who is the therapist here?")

R: Do not think. Listen!

E: All right. Very good. I know the body, Athor, is getting very tired. I would like to ask one more question and then we are going to stop for today. This is a question that I feel intuitively that many eons ago I also came from one of the outer galaxies, one of the other constellations, and I would like to see if you can give me any further insight on that, Athor.

R: Please state your name, your full name.

E: Evelyn Fuqua; at birth, Annie Evelyn Bassett.

R: Yes. It is seen that your soul, as it were, your soul essence, originated from the Celestial Kingdom. There is much light, much movement, much dancing, much joy. The land, the place, the realm of the fairies, the nymphs, the sprites, the Devas. You are well versed in that realm.

E: Thank you. Thank you very much. We need to let the body rest so when I count to five, slowly begin to come back into full waking consciousness.

R: It is seen that with the name change you have added a masculine vibration. Not that it was lacking within, but you have concreted much with this change. It has been your grounding.

E: Yes. It certainly has been my grounding. (My husband was a geologist.) Very much. Thank you. As you prepare to come back and open your eyes, I call on the link here between myself and Athor to give Athor some of these grounding qualities. I am often more grounded, in fact, than I wish to be, and perhaps we can exchange some of the energies

Athor has. Let me contribute some of my grounding energy to Athor. Let that exchange of energy help the body cope better here on the Earth with the gravity pull and all of the Earthly difficulties of the body.

R: The body feels the energy.

E: I give thanks for this session today in bringing through all this with the help of the Higher Essence of both of us. And so now, when I count to five, let Athor come back into this body and be well-grounded, being able to cope here on Earth, in the practical, mundane-type things that help us here in this existence, knowing that all of the wonderful memories come from the other planes, but that we are both here to help raise the vibrations of the Earth and in order to do this, we both need healthy bodies, bodies that are able to function well here on Earth. One, two, three, four, five.

At the end of this session, Rose and I just looked at each other and laughed. We did this spontaneously after many subsequent sessions. It was our method of breaking the tremendous tension that built up during the time so much of this mind-boggling information came through. This session would seem to indicate that Athor is a S.E.E. (Soul Exchange Entity) but neither Rose nor I was totally ready to believe this yet.

I had even more difficulty believing that I came from the Celestial Kingdom. That was a lovely thought, but all of this was beginning to sound more and more like fantasy to me. It was at this point that I began to wonder about my own sanity. I wanted to believe all this, but at another level I kept telling myself it could not be true. I had never heard of any case of a Soul Exchange in a child as young as Rose. How could I possibly believe this?

Then on Sunday night, February 12, six days after the Soul Exchange hypnotherapy session, I had an experience that changed my life in many ways. I was taking my usual walk with our dog, Pie' (P-A'), a large shepherd-collie mix so strong it was impossible to put him on a leash without his pulling me down. Since Pie' liked to roam, we always went for a walk at night when there were few cars on the street.

I had plenty of time to look up at the stars because I often stopped to give Pie' time to "explore" before we moved on. The night of February 12 was rather overcast, with some of the valley fog moving in. We live in an area with twenty-four one-acre lots, which gives this particular area a country flavor, although the entire perimeter around us has built up since we moved to Rocklin, a suburban area near Sacramento.

As Pie' and I approached a cul-de-sac about three lots past our house, I looked up at the sky and saw dozens of lights. They were all identical, like fat exclamation points without the dots. These formations seemed to be dancing around in the sky in no particular pattern. As I began walking down the cul-de-sac, I continued to look up in complete awe and joy for what was probably about ten minutes, although I was completely unaware of time. Then suddenly, in the western sky, there were only four lights circling counterclockwise, meeting in the center. This spiral motion kept repeating over and over again. Time stood still as I gazed in wonderment at this amazing display in the sky.

I finally realized I was getting quite chilly. Pie' had become bored and was standing by my side. I told him how wonderful all of this was, but he was totally oblivious to what I was observing. So much for my psychic dog. I decided that I wanted my husband to see this, partly because it was so remarkable, but also because I wanted another human being to verify that the lights were real and not just an hallucination. I telepathically asked the lights to follow me home.

I turned and walked quickly back without looking up. When I looked up again, there were the lights, spiraling around, then meeting in the center right in front of my house. I quickly went in the house to ask my husband to come out. He came out, looked at the lights briefly, and remarked that they were probably searchlights. He tuned out my remark about the lights all over the sky at the beginning. This was typical of my scientific-minded husband and his simple explanation did not particularly concern me. At least he saw the lights, which was my objective. It was then 10:30. The pattern continued for some time, and I finally went into the house. When I came out again, about twenty minutes later, the lights had disappeared. I later saw searchlights in our area, but they were quite different from what I had seen.

Ever since that experience, I have pondered what it meant. When I attended the spring conference of A.P.R.T, Dr. Leo Sprinkle was the keynote speaker. Dr. Sprinkle is a former counseling psychologist and associate professor at the University of Wyoming, where for many years he organized annual conferences for UFO contactees.

I told Leo about my experience and asked him what he thought it meant. His response was, "What do you think it means?"

He indicated there was much symbolism in this particular experience, and that I would be the best person to interpret what it meant personally, a logical remark by a good psychologist. Although this was far from the typical UFO sighting, he thought it was definitely an extraterrestrial contact of some kind. At that time, my best explanation was that it was a confirmation that I was on the right track in my work with Athor and that it was all right to accept the information coming through her.

Since then, additional thoughts about the experience have occurred to me. I now sense that the lights spiraling around in a counterclockwise movement were symbolic of the fact that we all come from the same Source; we go out to various planets, planes, and dimensions to have the experiences the soul has decided upon after its separation from the Source and then we finally all go back to the same Source. The many lights dancing around at the beginning, I connect increasingly with the Celestial Realm where everyone is a being of Light and there is much joy as these lights dance about.

At the time of my sighting of these beautiful "Beings of Light," it did not seem strange to me that no one else was around. Because it was very overcast and cold, it was not a night when most people would want to be outside their homes. Usually, a few cars would go by during my walks but there were no cars that night, just my dog and myself. I somehow knew that this was an experience just for me. It was an awe-inspiring, extremely spiritual awakening.

This helped me a great deal in accepting my strange relationship with Athor—or Rose—or whoever she was. But neither she nor I was totally convinced that she was a S.E.E. Rose continued to have frequent, near-fatal attacks from heart fibrillation, which usually occurred during the early morning hours. She told me that she consciously forced her heart to keep beating.

When a therapist in Sacramento called and asked if he could observe some of my work, I thought of Athor. As a professional therapist, I could not allow someone to observe my regular fee-paying clients, but it would be valuable to get another therapist's input into the Athor case. Rose-Athor was in agreement. This turned out to be a mistake, however, since it proved to be a real setback for Rose.

It is seen that as the incoming spirit clothed in its particular and unique consciousness begins to enter the Earth plane dimension, it passes through many and various levels and frequencies wherein there are certain energies which are generated, and it magnetically attracts certain energies and frequencies unto itself to begin to, in a sense, clothe itself in grosser and grosser physical plane density. It first comes forth from what we term the Logoic Haven, wherein it resides upon its return before it returns fully to the Source.

Each and every soul which, whether it has been through your Earth plane dimension incarnation process or not, has periodic visitations, shall we say, to the Logoic Haven. Each galactic system within a certain Universe has a particular Logos and Logoic Haven wherein the souls from that galactic system and Universe all return at some point to the Logoic Haven before either reincarnating through the physical plane or coming forth in other frequencies. While residing in the Logoic Haven, the spiritual body recharges itself. It is in this place, or consciousness, that the spiritual body regenerates. For you see, as the physical body must regenerate through your mechanism of breathing and eating and ingesting water, so also must the spiritual body regenerate. So as the soul regenerates, it is almost, in very simplistic terms, like recharging your battery.

— Athor, November 10, 1990

Chapter 11

Exorcism

Reverend Michael Darby is not a licensed therapist, but he does past-life regression therapy, and he's had extensive experience in depossession and exorcism. I do "Spirit Releasement" therapy, which is a more gentle and loving approach than the authoritative exorcism style of dealing with entities. But then, I have never had a case of what I considered true possession—just attached entities which, nevertheless, were often seriously affecting the life of the client.

True possession, in my opinion, is rare. This often results in what is known as Multiple Personalities. As it turned out, the approach used with Rose-Athor was closely akin to the "exorcism" approach depicted in movies. This may not be apparent from the contents of the transcript, but it was quite clear from the tone of voice used by Rev. Darby that he was using this kind of approach.

I had described Rose's case to Rev. Darby before his session with us. I told him I thought that Rose was a S.E.E, but I was still not sure. He expressed the opinion that a Soul Exchange is not possible, therefore, this was probably a case of possession. I told him I really did not agree with that theory; however, there was still some element of doubt in my mind.

With Rose's permission, I agreed to let him participate in a session. I would begin the session, then ask him to join in if and when I thought it was appropriate.

I began by going back to the time of the "Soul Exchange" to get clarification regarding the silver cord. Rev. Darby had expressed doubt about the S.E.E. experience because, from his studies, he had been under the impression that the silver cord disconnects at death. He did not believe there could be a soul transference if this cord did disconnect. He also questioned what happened to the auric field during a so-called Soul Exchange. It was at this point, during a discussion of the auric field, that I asked Rev. Darby to take over the questioning, since at that time I was not thoroughly aware of the different bodies of the auric field.

Hypnosis Session, April 1, 1989

E: Evelyn

A: Athor

D: Darby

E: And now you're back at the age when all of this is happening. Tell me what is happening.

A: (Deep breathing—nothing is said.)

E: Much is happening in your body. Can you tell me what is happening in your mind?

A: (Very quick, labored breathing—sounds of pain and moaning.) There is something coming out of my skin.

E: Something coming out of your skin. All right. Take a deep breath. Let it come out. Let it come out. Experience it. (Athor's breathing quiets down considerably.) All right now, relax.

A: It looks like me.

E: It's like you?

A: Looks like me.

E: Tell me more about that. Are you seeing something outside of yourself that looks like you?

A: Yes! There's two beings that are taking me away.

E: All right. What is happening in your body now that this has been taken away?

A: I'm not in my body, but I don't know where I am. It's like I ... I don't know how to explain it. I know I'm not the one that looks like me that they're taking away. But I feel ... I don't feel anything.

E: But you're thinking!

A: Yes, but . . .

E: I'd like for you to look down on this body that is talking right now.

A: It's not the body that is talking!

E: What is it that's talking?

A: Which body are you referring to? The one of three years and two months?

E: Yes.

A: The body is not talking. The body's not talking . . .

E: I need some clarification on that. When you say "I am talking," who is "I"?

A: (Deep sigh.) I am Athor!

E: Now Athor, we have met before. I'd like to ask you a question that I've never asked before, but I'd like to get an explanation. From what we know, if a person's spirit disconnects from their body, the silver cord also disconnects. If you're saying that the Rose spirit is no longer there, can you explain how you got there?

A: (Deep sigh.)

E: What has happened with the silver cord? Did that go with Rose when they took her body away? I don't understand.

A: What is not presently understood here on this planet is that in the process of the so-called Soul Exchange, that which is transmitted is not the actual total spiritual entity or essence, but a level of what you would term one of the other—or in many cases—several of the other bodies, or vehicles, as you presently term them. In this case of this vehicle presently in this room at this time, the transference which occurred was effected on the third, fourth, and fifth levels of the auric field.

(At this point I exchanged places with Rev. Darby and indicated that he should take over the questioning. All of his part of the transcript was stated in a very authoritative tone of voice. He is obviously challenging the statements made by Athor.)

D: Which vehicles of consciousness are you using?

A: The fourth and fifth, and occasionally the third.

D: You say the fourth and fifth. Would you describe them to me in a more definitive way that I might understand? Would it be the mental self? Would it be the emotional self, the spiritual self? Which dimension or level are we discussing?

A: (Deep sigh.) We are dealing herein with the level which you term the causal body, as well as that which you term the mental bodies. Occasionally there has been contact and transference through the emotional vehicles as well.

D: So it's not just the fourth and fifth. It would be the third, fourth, and fifth. Is that how you would refer to it?

A: Primarily the fourth and fifth, occasionally the third.

D: How do you connect into this physical vehicle that you might use it?

A: Through the solar plexus chakra.

D: Mmmm. Are you using the vehicle of the brain?

A: At times.

D: How do you do that?

A: There's a connection in through the back of the head near the base of the medulla oblongata.

D: When you say a connection, what type of connection are you referring to?

A: A ray—an energy transmission that is hooked to this unit.

D: What color is it?

A: Silvery white.

D: Do you create that, or is it created by someone else?

A: This is transmitted from the levels wherein we originate.

D: Where do you originate?

A: (Deep sigh.) That which you term as the constellation Sirius.

D: And why are you here?

A: (Deep sigh.) We are here to effect an interplanetary exchange of energies from these levels, for which purpose there has been a necessity to ground through a physical vehicle on this plane.

D: Mmmm. And upon whose authority are you functioning?

A: [Sigh.] Those of us who are termed the High Council of the Elders.

D: Mmmm. And do you believe in God?

A: Indeed!

D: Explain God to me, please! Your concept of God.

A: (Sigh.) God, as you term the word, is the interpenetrating energy which imbues ... both imbues and surrounds all that which is in existence.

D: And do you gain authority from God to come to this planet and assume use of this physical body in the way that you have done?

A: This is presupposing your concept of God. This is not speaking of God which we understand. In presupposing and using your concept of God—

D: How do you know what my concept of God is? Are you saying my concept or are you talking about the concept of the planet?

A: The planet.

D: I understand. Okay. Now, I want to ask you a couple more questions. Do you believe that God is love?

A: Indeed!

D: And do you believe that God manifests through beings in loving actions, deeds, thoughts, words?

A: At times—not exclusively.

D: Okay. Now, I'm going to ask you a more pointed question. You've taken control of certain centers within this individual's body, but it has caused this individual a great deal of grief and problems. That's not of God! Would you explain that to me, please?

A: (Deep sigh.) That again is presupposing the concept of God which exists upon the face of this planet.

D: But you just said to me that God is love.

A: Yes, but we have also stated that at times it is expressed in that manner. Do not put words where they do not belong.

D: Well, the same might be said for this communication we're having.what gives you the right?

A: We are using your concept from which you are functioning. You do not understand what we are saying.

D: Well, I understand words! Now, can you communicate to me so that I might understand?

A: (Deep sigh.) What is it you wish to know?

D: What gives you the right to take control of another person's body and bring to that person years of grief, of disease, of trouble, of emotional problems? What gives you that right? And why do you take this position that it's your God and we perceive, presuppose, some other God? What gives you that right? You bring illness, sickness, hurt, harm to this person's body that you've invaded. What gives you that right? Please answer that!

A: (Deep sigh.) We do not perceive it in that fashion, as we are not used to dealing with physical vehicles. If that is the case—then we will make adjustments.

D: Gibberish! What gives you the right to invade a person's body and cause them illness and sickness and heartache and years of suffering? If you come from a God of love, answer that to me!

A: (Deep sigh.) As has been stated, we do not perceive it as such.

D: How do you perceive it?

A: (Deep sigh; pause.)

D: You're lost for words? I'm not, and I'll tell you how I perceive it!

A: Go on.

D: You have violated this person's privacy and this person's right to continue their progress in God's love and Light. You have violated everything that is sacred and good in God's love and Light! Be gone with you!

A: (Chuckle.)

D: Someone else's unhappiness makes you laugh?

A: No, you're assuming a position of authority which seeks—

D: If you have that right, then I do, too! You assumed the position of authority of taking possession of someone else's body! You don't have that right or, on the other hand, explain to me what gives you that right through God's law as we can universally understand it. That makes sense to you, doesn't it? Or does it?

A: Please state your understanding or definition of God's law.

D: Do unto others as you would have them do to you in love, goodness—in justice, in beauty, in truth. You want someone to come and invade your body eventually—take control of you and cause you illness, cause you heartache?

A: There is no body. (Athor comes from a realm where there are no bodies as humans know them.)

D: There is no body? What's the one you're talking through right now? That's a body! At least, I perceive it as a body. Am I functioning under an illusion?

A: You are speaking to me, and as the "me," there is no body.

D: Well, get out of that body and talk to me! Can you do that?

A: No. (See further explanation of "no body" in discussion of Rev. Darby's conclusions.)

D: I can! If you come from a higher dimension, demonstrate that to me. If you are this benevolent intelligence who comes from some other part of the Universe for some reason we don't know yet—we haven't asked you that question—then demonstrate something good and just and beautiful and true and lovely through God to us right now. Give us some wisdom. Step out of that body and communicate with me! I can see you!

A: As you wish. (long pause)

D: Rose, I want you, with your own mind now, to create a beautiful violet Light energy right where I touch you. Create that with your own mind and then begin to bathe yourself mentally in this beautiful and sacred violet Light energy. Just mentally wash yourself…feel this wonderful essence of Light and love as this energy flows in, through, and around every part of your being. Strengthening your mind…cleansing and purifying your mind…strengthening your spirit…strengthening your emotional body. Do you see the violet Light energy, Rose?

A: Hmmm.

D: How does that feel to you?

A: I don't have any feeling about it.

D: Tell me when you see it. Do you see it as a light like comes out of a light bulb, or do you see it as a moving energy?

A: (Deep sigh.) Well, I see it in front of me and all around me.

D: Do you see it within yourself, in your mind's eye?

A: Right now I can only see it as the scene where I am.

D: Where are you?

A: It's a strange place—sort of like a mixture between a desert and a jungle.

D: Between a desert and a jungle? What colors do you see around?

A: There's some strange plant-like objects that are brown, and some are yellow and pink-green, but they look like fake flowers.

D: I want you to go to the top of a very high mountain, preferably in India or Tibet. I want you to stand on top of this mountain at peace with yourself—at peace with God.

A: I'm sitting down on a chair.

D: On top of the mountain?

A: Yeah.

D: How do you feel there?

A: Like I'm waiting for someone.

D: Just above you is a beautiful golden Light energy that's descending on you. I want you, with your own mind, to reach up and pull that energy into and around every part of you.

A: I do, and there's a dove.

D: Good. And how does that golden Light energy feel to you?

A: I still have the feeling of waiting for someone.

D: Hmmm. But how does the golden Light energy feel to you if you pull that into and around every part of your being? Tell me what it feels like—golden flame energy.

A: Warm.

D: I want you to be a little more intense with that right now. I'm going to touch your forehead here and I want you to concentrate intently upon golden Light energy. I want you to pull that in, through, and around every part of your being with your own mind. Now tell me how that feels.

A: The same—just warm. I don't have any strong feelings about it.

D: Okay. Let me ask you a pointed question. Do you feel just a little more aware right now in this golden flame energy?

A: No.

D: Are you still sitting in the chair on top of the mountain?

A: Mmm-hmm.

D: I want you to look just behind you. There's a pathway there. Do you see that pathway?

A: Well, if you put it there, it's there.

D: It's there! Do you see it?

A: No, because I have the feeling you're putting it there. I can't see it.

D: I can't put it there. You're on top of the mountain. Just look behind you to your left from where you're sitting.

A: All I see over there is a dark shape.

D: A dark shape?

A: Mmm-hmm.

D: How dark, and what kind of shape?

A: Very dark!

D: What kind of shape?

A: Like a Yeti.

D: Mmm-hmm.

A: Like an ape man.

D: Like an ape man. Okay. I want you to walk over toward this Yeti and just direct this beautiful golden Light energy to this Yeti in love, and you'll see that he will go away in peace. Just surround him in this beautiful golden Light and send him your love from deep within your heart. Did he leave?

A: He turned . . .

D: Okay. How do you see the pathway while you're looking over there? There's a beautiful pathway there.

A: (Sighing.) I just see the forest.

D: Just walk over toward the forest and eventually, as you walk over there, you'll see....

A: There's a trail...

D: There, that's it! It's a pathway! I want you to walk down that pathway. Each step that you take, you'll be deeper and deeper relaxed as this beautiful gold Light energy continues to enfold you. Just walk along comfortably. Do not anticipate anything—do not anticipate anyone. Just walk along comfortably and enjoy yourself. Enjoy the beauty around you. Someone with whom it's important that you meet and talk today is going to make their presence known to you. As soon as they do, let me know.

A: (Pause) There's no one there.

D: Just continue walking.

A: I'm at a stream.

D: Walk across the stream.

A: No, there's a boat.

D: There's a what?

A: A boat.

D: A boat? Okay. Would you go across in the boat?

A: Well, it's going downstream, not across.

D: Good—go downstream. Go to the other side.

A: No. Now we're getting to a waterfall like Niagara Falls.

D: Okay. How do you feel?

A: Well, then let me tell you what's happening here. (chuckle) Uh-hmm! The boat goes over the end, and I'm caught on a branch hanging there. I'm climbing up on the branch, and I sit and watch the water and listen to it.

D: And how do you feel about that?

A: I like the sound of the water, the rushing water.

D: Are you frightened at all?

A: No, but I feel like—not a gnome—but one of those woodsy creatures, a nymph or a sprite or something.

D: Aha.

A: Sitting on the branch.

D: Okay. I want you to leave that scene, Rose. Go back to the top of the mountain—just sit there, relax. I want you to see yourself again completely enveloped in beautiful golden Light energy. And you are at peace with yourself. You are at peace with God. And I want you to perceive yourself perfectly balanced. I want you to create an image of yourself perfectly balanced—mentally, emotionally, spiritually. And as you create that image of yourself, I'm going to step to the background here and let Evelyn guide you. Continue to pour this beautiful golden Light upon this image of yourself—perfect, perfect balance—mentally, emotionally, and spiritually. All right, Rose, how are you feeling now?

A: (Sigh) Well, I don't like the image. (laughs) It's like from the tarot cards—the image of "The Fool." I'm standing on one foot—both feet on different ends of a scale and neither one is going up or down. But it looks like a very powerful man! Doesn't look like me, and—

E: I want you to move up into your Higher Self and look at this—getting in touch with your spirits and guides and looking down at this experience today from the Higher Self. And I'd like the Higher Self part of you to give some insight into how this experience has affected you. What is your feeling about it? How has it helped? What has been the perception from the Higher Spirit part of you of what you have just experienced?

A: (Deep sigh)

E: Has this changed anything for you?

A: No. I hear it has been but a mental exercise designed to distract.

E: Is then your feeling, also looking at this from the higher viewpoint, that this is not a possession-type experience that you went through at an early age that you started out with today? Was that a possession as we generally think of spirits coming in and entering people's bodies?

A: I hear "yes" and "no." Only in the sense as you perceive it as being an invasion can it be classified in your terminology as possession. However, it has been stated previously that this being has allowed the entry, the exchange to occur. For the prior consciousness wished to vacate.

E: I'd like to go back to the earlier question because that was not clear to me. When the spirit of Rose—that you state was taken from the body—did the silver cord disconnect and go with that body? Did it disconnect from the physical body?

A: (Deep sigh) You, in your present understanding, meaning people, see or view that there is but one cord that links the vehicles to the physical body. What you do not as yet understand is that there are many, many layers within that cord, as it were. In effect, there are other so-called cords within that cord. The sum total of the cord was not disconnected, as it were. However, on the other levels and layers, as has been stated previously, there were disconnections within that cord.

E: The issue that was brought up today by Rev. Darby was a very valid issue that we have dealt with before—and if indeed, Athor, you are from Sirius and you are down here in her body, and this has been a mutual exchange, you must help Rose deal with the physical vehicle. We still do not have any definitive information on how she is going to handle this problem we talked about last time, that she, also being an Earth being, has become attached to the Earth and does not want to leave the Earth at this point. And you, Athor, let me ask you this: Do you want to remain here on Earth for a period of time, or do you want to leave this Earth?

A: (Deep sigh) It is difficult to accurately transmit a sufficient explanation when you use the terminology, "Do you wish to remain on Earth?" There is no singular, identifiable presence that is encased, as it were, in this physical body. Thus, the nature of the questioning is such that it does not permit a readily available answer.

(We later discovered that Athor is an aspect of a group soul.)

E: Let me see if I can simplify this, then. If Rose's body dies, according to the terminology that we use here on Earth, the physical body dies because of all the chaos that has been caused in it by your dwelling there. What would happen to you? Where would you go?

A: (Deep sigh) The energy which is presently connected through this physical vehicle has not a commonly understood identity, as such, as you are familiar with upon this plane. The energy is a non-personal transmission designed to provide a link through a physical vehicle to the planet Earth for the sole intent and purpose of bridging the gap, as it were, between the so-called higher dimensions, as you refer to them, and the physical expressions herein upon this plane. It has been found—it has been seen— that there is a necessity to ground these frequencies into and through the physical plane and dimension. This can only be effected through a suitable physical vehicle.

E: Is Rose any longer a suitable vehicle because of her physical problems?

A: (Deep sigh) There is a point well taken here, in that on an individualized, personalized level there is indeed a reality, as it were, which we have not considered. It has been seen as a result of this exchange that a further transmission is necessary to balance the effects of upheaval which have herein occurred in this physical vehicle.

E: What kind of transmission is this going to be? Will it be a physical transmission of energy of some sort coming into her body? Will it be messages coming to her on how to deal with this? Explain the transmission part.

A: (Deep sigh) It is seen that as she goes through her daily meditation of realigning the chakras, of cleaning, cleansing, emptying out the chakra fields, the transmission will occur through the innermost molecular frequency, radiating gradually outward from within. You, upon this plane, have consistently believed (sigh) that—energy—I see the double helix over here (pointing to the left), and then I see like a sixteen-strand helix over here (pointing to the right). The image of the double helix is like a flat, one-dimensional plane. This thing has length, height, width, and depth and the whole thing—it's sitting over here. It's like trying to say, "This is the difference!"

E: Which is the Earth and which is the higher dimensions? The one on the left is the Earth?

A: Yes. This is wherein we speak.

E: Okay, and the sixteen strand helix is of higher dimensions. All right. I'm sure the body is tired.

A: No, surprisingly not. (chuckles)

E: Good, good. You've been through quite a bit here! All right, I need to stop very soon, but I would like to ask if you have any final messages you'd like to bring through today. Address anything you wish to address. (I count backwards from ten to one to induce a deeper trance state.) Are there any further messages?

A: (Addressing Rev. Darby) It is wise to remember that though one has studied much and feels that they are indeed an expert in a certain area or field, there is much, much more to be learned which has not as yet been tapped. Do not perceive that you are the sole authority and source. There is a much greater picture to all which occurs upon the face of this planet. Do not assume that your laws, your understanding, and your regulations cover the entire spectrum of reality. Such is by far not the case. That is all.

E: All right. Thank you, and we're going to stop today. When I count to three, feel refreshed…

A: I do.

E: Relaxed, energized. Letting the body completely be able to carry through with all the cleansing you've talked about today. With the knowledge that you will be getting better.

But, despite a temporary surge of energy, Rose did not get better. She called me the next day to say she had experienced much emotional trauma after leaving my office and was deeply depressed. She was affected by the dense energy coming from Rev. Darby. "I feel as if I have been mentally raped!"

As I listened to the interchange between Rose-Athor and Rev. Darby, I was aware that she was becoming deeply upset, but I also knew that if, in fact, there were any possibility that Rose was possessed by Athor, it would be necessary to be forceful and totally authoritative in order to have the entity leave. I kept silent to see where all of this would go. It was apparent that Rev. Darby was becoming confused by Rose-Athor's responses. I am sure he was beginning to realize that this did not fit the usual pattern of a case of possession.

Actually, I was rather amused because I had felt confused many times because of Rose-Athor's obstinate refusal to go along with what I thought was best for her. Now she was doing the same thing with another therapist. I observed the deterioration of the session. Athor was obviously just playing a game with Rev. Darby toward the end. I think she wasn't tired because she got the better of him, which rather delighted her. However, there was enough of the "exorcism" approach to take its toll on her emotionally.

Rev. Darby called me the next day to check on how Rose was doing. He expressed much concern about her but continued to hold the opinion that this was a case of possession. After the session, he decided that Rose was possessed by an entity from a lower astral plane and by elementals. Although I thought he meant well, I was upset with him and was not in a frame of mind to question him about his conclusions. He had reached this decision through a number of factors.

The connection was made through the emotional and mental bodies as well as the causal body. He had told me that if indeed S.E.E.s do exist, they would come in only through the causal body. My understanding now is that the mechanics of the exchange vary with each case. There is no one way that an exchange occurs, but at that time my experience with Walk-Ins was limited to this one case so I was in no position to argue the point.

The many statements Athor made indicating that "there is no body" were probably confusing and misunderstood by Rev. Darby. As in most of the hypnosis sessions, Athor was channeling her Higher Self, and, from the viewpoint of the Higher Self, Athor has no body. We found out later that Athor is an aspect of a group soul from Sirius and as such has no physical body. Athor is an entity of pure Light.

Usually, if I'm doing a Spirit Releasement session with a client and the client says, "I have no body," I assume that a spirit attachment is speaking and not the core personality in the body. It's completely understandable that Rev. Darby was confused by this case. Athor has great difficulty in bonding to her body, since having a body, particularly one which gives her many problems, is a new experience for her.

Many of her physical problems are probably related to her rejection of her body. It seems logical that if S.E.E.s have previously had physical bodies, the Soul Exchange process and Earth existence are much easier. We later established that this is the first incarnation in a physical body for this aspect of the Athor soul.

Another factor that may have affected Rev. Darby's diagnosis was the dark form Rose said was a Yeti (Bigfoot). We later learned that Rose had a past-life experience in the Himalayas with the Yeti. This may have been a glimpse of that episode. Rose also talked about being caught on a branch when the boat she was in went over a waterfall. "Ah—the boat goes over the end, and I'm caught on a branch, hanging there, and I'm climbing up on the branch, and I sit and watch the water."

After more questions, she stated, "I feel like—not a gnome—but one of those woodsy creatures—a nymph or a sprite or something sitting on the branch." This would indicate an elemental or nature spirit. Rose, in fact, does on occasion have conversations with nature spirits. However, she tries to avoid them because she feels that she does not have the time for "this nonsense."

There is a possibility that some kind of elemental or nature spirit was in Rose-Athor's physical body at the time of the exorcism and may have been released as a result of this session. However, the main issue was the nature of the Athor personality. It was clear that Athor was definitely still in the body. After this session I was more convinced than ever that Athor was indeed a S.E.E. We needed to accept that fact and get on with the therapy.

After this rather devastating experience, however, Athor did not return for any more sessions for several weeks. She apparently had lost some of her faith in me as a therapist because I allowed Rev. Darby to work with her. I was also upset with myself at the time and questioned the wisdom of allowing it to happen. As I write this nearly two years later, however, I now feel this was a necessary step in the therapy.

It's appropriate at this point to include some discussion about Multiple Personalities (MP). From a traditional therapeutic point of view, this might be seriously considered as a diagnosis for Rose. However, I have a different interpretation of Multiple Personalities from that of the usual therapist. I believe that many cases of MP are really a form of entity possession. I had never believed that Rose was possessed. However, several prior sessions with Rose had been directed toward finding out if the entity channeling through Rose was an attached entity.

There are many degrees of entity problems, all the way from attachments, which can cause many problems, to firmly entrenched entities whose presence is like a possession. We usually think of someone being "possessed" by an evil entity as in the movie, "The Exorcist." This is quite rare, although the phenomenon does exist.

On the other hand, many of us have had attached entities at some time in our lives. They are simply Earthbound spirits who do not have any spiritual beliefs in a life after death. Therefore, they stay on the lower astral plane, often attaching to anyone who has a weakened aura, such as people with addictions, psychics who do not protect themselves adequately, children who have had tremendous trauma in their lives, or any of us who have available openings in our auric fields.

Children who are abused often have a pattern of leaving their bodies (out-of-body travel or astral travel) during the time of abuse. This is one mechanism to help them survive repeated trauma. The core personality often has no memory of the abuse because that personality is not in the body at the time of the abuse. The already weakened aura makes the child's body an ideal place for Earthbound spirits to enter. If enough of these spirits come into the child's body, the core personality becomes progressively weaker while the entities become stronger—strong enough to take over the body totally at times, thus resulting in a so-called Multiple Personality.

These entities or spirits actually help the child to survive early in life because the abuse is directed toward several personalities, not just one. The core personality may be out of the body many times during the abuse; therefore, when the child becomes an adult, the core personality may be able to function in an apparently normal manner, since it has no conscious memory of the abuse. What causes the problem is the frequent change in personality when one of the entities takes control. This results in periods of time when the core personality has no conscious knowledge of the actions of the other personalities, which constitutes a very disruptive way of life.

The Diagnostic Statistical Evaluation of Mental Disorders (DSM-III) gives the following criteria for diagnosis of Multiple Personality:

(1) The individual has two or more distinct personalities, each of which is dominant at a particular time;

(2) The personality that is dominant at any particular time determines the individual's behavior;

(3) Each individual personality is complex and integrated, with its own unique behavior patterns and social relationships.

Spirit possessions deeply entrenched since childhood can cause all of these characteristics.

In a sense, much of the therapy to this point had been an attempt to determine if Rose were a case of Multiple Personality, although I had not used that terminology. I knew she had the usual childhood pattern that can result in Multiple Personality. She certainly had the abuse, and she had much conscious experience of communication in "altered states" which to her, as a child, was quite "normal." I believe now that it was only because of being an extraterrestrial that she was able to survive without becoming a so-called Multiple Personality.

Her behavior did not fit any of the criteria for a MP. Her personality was always consistent. There appeared to be a strong core personality that never varied, except with normal mood changes depending, in her case, on her current physical condition. I never saw her exhibit anything other than rational behavior.

Although Athor seemed to be a different personality when she was in a trance state, there was no sense of another personality taking over the body, and there was always the awareness that the body was in a trance state. From an analytical point of view, using strictly DSM criteria, Rose is not a Multiple Personality, but this was such a puzzling case that I wanted to be sure. Even if Athor were just an entity attachment and not a true possession, this in itself could cause serious physical problems.

I was still quite unsure about my diagnosis of Rose as a S.E.E. when we had the session with Rev. Darby. I would have liked to have discussed the case with some other licensed professionals but I knew of no one, not even those in the Association of Past-Life Research and Therapies directory who had experience with this kind of phenomenon. In retrospect, this session seems to have been a necessary step, although at the time I did not perceive it as such. Certainly Athor did not take this view.

After Athor read this chapter, she called me later one evening to say that the following information had "come" to her.

Multiple Personalities: Three Types

(1) Spirit entrance (as described in this chapter).
(2) Fragmentation within the psyche itself to cope and experience different aspects simultaneously. The terror and trauma of early experiences in this case creates a fragmentation within both the mental and the emotional bodies, creating a "splitting off" or an "opening" as it were, wherein the memory banks of both the mental and emotional bodies are activated in haphazard fashion and the personality of that life cycle

becomes "infused" with fragments of "past-life personalities" as well as "creations" of personalities from the subconscious mind and present conditions and environment.

(3) The third type is one wherein the basic ovoid shape of the auric field is greatly compromised, allowing thought forms and beings from the elemental realm to enter and "play" in that person's energy field—taking on human form and experiencing human experiences without actually inhabiting a physical form through the incarnative processes.

Each of these three types requires a different healing approach; though the basic method of attempting some type of harmonious integration works somewhat better in some than in others, depending on the initial causation. Psychological integration works best with the second type of Multiple Personality. The first and third can be aided greatly by a combined approach of assisting the client in recognizing the causative factor (which requires the expertise of a reputable clairvoyant who can "see" the energy patterns and methods of entry, etc.), and then using a variety of methods, including some form of Spirit Releasement and auric work, as well as psychological techniques geared toward integrating the mental and emotional bodies.

I would add to this information provided by Athor that, since Multiple Personalities are extremely difficult to treat, it would be wise for professionals to consider the services of a competent clairvoyant to determine which type a patient is, thus giving clearer insight into an effective treatment.

"Second encounter with extraterrestrials: The vehicle (child, Rose) is playing, in what appears to be a sand area, a sandbox. Two beings are present, one on each side, and the vehicle is rather pleasantly surprised that they are once more visiting. The one on the right has a staff-like object, with which he proceeds to draw a symbol in the sand, and the vehicle is told that this is the symbol to the gateway to Infinite Intelligence. The being proceeds to move the staff in a circle about the heads of all three present and communicates the concept that it is "here," meaning surrounding and interpenetrating all within the circle.

"It then points the staff-like object to the sky and says that it is "there" (pointing to the sky). And then, it most vehemently thumps the ground with the staff-like object and indicates that it is "here," thus indicating that there is nothing exempt from Infinite Intelligence ... These beings are the guardians of the gateway which oftentimes precede the passage of what you term your 'Walk-In' transitions. They come from various frequencies and levels, as they must have the capacity and understanding to bring forth sufficient knowledge to the exiting being to allow it to exit appropriately."

— *Athor, March 19, 1990*

Chapter 12

Rose Explains

S ome time elapsed before I had another hypnosis session with Athor. Aside from the negative effects on Athor of the exorcism session, I was busy preparing for the spring A.P.R.T. conference. As program chair, I had numerous letters to write and phone calls to make prior to the conference. Then there were letters of appreciation to write afterwards to the various speakers. This, in addition to my private practice and post-retirement job with my former school district, kept me too busy to be very much involved with Athor for quite a while.

By the time we had another therapy session, we were both convinced that Rose was really Athor and that this truly was a Soul Exchange. The next session began to give more information regarding the "Divine Essence."

Before beginning our session, Athor asked that I direct her to go into a helix. She had seen flashes of a helix in her meditations and thought it might be a useful method of getting information to help her with her physical problems.

Hypnosis Session, June 12, 1989

E: Evelyn
A: Athor
E: Now go back again to the Soul Exchange when this body was three years, two months old. Let's get in touch with exactly what's happening.
A: The body is out of control. It would seem that the whole or full force of the energy would shatter the auric sheath completely, thus terminating the physical vessel. Adjustments must be made to only bring down one-third of the energy frequency. The system is not adequately equipped to handle the electrical frequency.
E: Where is the body of Rose?
A: It has been taken to the Base Center, the Mother Ship, as it were. The body is not equipped, and it is difficult for the adjustments to be made, as infusion of this frequency is indeed foreign to this physical vehicle.
E: What part of the body is making the exchange of energy? How is it being performed?

A: There are many levels with which we are working here. The heart chakra area is one; the solar plexus is another. Then we must also make adaptations and changes in the crown chakra and the brow chakra, as the normal visionary processes which have heretofore been dampened in the average human being must be opened. Yet it is seen that, again, the full force of the energy and the full expression of the energy is not possible through the vehicle as it presently exists.

E: Were the beings aware that this would be true, that it could not be a full exchange?

A: It was hoped that the energy would be received accordingly. However, the awareness was there that the possibility was great that the physical vehicle could not accommodate such energetic transference as this type has not been effective previously. It was to be seen to which stage the human evolutionary cellular component—how far they had gotten.

E: How is this experiment different from the usual Soul Exchange experience?

A: The usual S.E.E. experience is one in which the full range of energies is not present on this physical plane. Of course, we also see here that this is also the case. However, in the so-called normal Soul Exchange situation, there is only a transference between the mental and causal bodies and energies, which allows the being who exchanges souls to realign rather effortlessly, as it were, if necessary to allow for a transition and a change for another to come in.

Herein we see the attempt has been made to bond and, at the time of this transference, that the physical vehicle cannot accommodate such frequencies completely and fully. Thus we have what this being has referred to as a deep inner state of frustration, as though everything were racing at speeds millions of miles greater than the physical capacity would allow.

E: Why was this particular vehicle, known as Rose, chosen for this experiment?

A: It was felt that the preparation was sufficient to accommodate these energies.

E: Are we speaking of past-life preparation?

A: Yes.

E: How is it possible for Rose-Athor to remember past lives when she has this other energy in her? Is there some remnant of Rose still with her?

A: The cellular makeup of the physical vehicle is such that the transformation has not been effected on the cellular, physical level. That which is yet of the Earth plane remnant has not been transferred, as it were. So there is a division of sorts between that which we term the lower and the higher energies or frequencies—that being just those which vibrate at a higher or lower rate of speed.

E: Am I correct in interpreting that only one-third of this physical vehicle has been transferred to these higher energies?

A: At the time of three years and two months, such was the case. However, at the approximate time between eighteen and nineteen and a half years, another change was effected in which it would seem that the vehicle accommodated two-thirds of the energy heretofore actually transferred.

E: Take a deep breath, and let's go to that time between eighteen and nineteen and a half years old and see if there was a specific time when this transfer was accelerated.

A: Yes. It was a time when the vehicle was told she was going on a trip. It lasted approximately six hours in Earth time, in which the vehicle was given the choice to come back to the physical or to go on beyond the physical. It was at this time the consciousness chose to return to the physical vehicle, as it had not yet discovered why it was on Earth.

E: I want you to go back to that time and go to that specific experience and see how that acceleration of the energy exchange took place. At that point, where did the body go?

A: The body was physically on the bed in the college dormitory.

E: Yes. I remember that incident. Okay, then how did that take place? Tell me more about it.

A: The vehicle was looking to find the full essence of God, and it traveled through the planes and dimensions in the search. When it reached the point of no return, wherein the choice must be made whether to continue the physical incarnation or not, the vehicle decided, the consciousness decided, to return to the vehicle.

E: We're speaking then of the astral body that traveled these other dimensions. Is that correct?

A: Yes.

E: The actual exchange of further cosmic energy of this higher vibratory rate, did that occur when the consciousness came back in the body? At what point did that actually occur?

A: It was given when the vehicle had the experience of being on the mountain top in this trip, and being seated at a table where there were three chairs and viewing herself as sitting on the one chair for supper or dinner, as it were. That's when the vehicle was given the "golden key" and the "pearl" which was the time the energy was transmitted through the symbolic representation of the "key" and the "pearl."

When the consciousness awoke to the physical dimension, it had opened a physical center in the brain which permitted the physical brain to translate incoming data from all other physical brains. Thus the vehicle was able to hear other people's minds, word for word, and the vehicle could not adapt sufficiently to the opening, which was but a natural consequence of the effect of increased levels of energy and a telepathic transference. However, the physical part of the vehicle, which has not yet been transfigured, as it were, could not deal with this influx of energy and it chose to shut this down.

E: Is that potential still there if the vehicle were to choose to open up again?

A: Yes, indeed.

E: Is the vehicle able to do that at will? Not as a constant thing which the human body could not stand, but can the Higher Self of this vehicle do that when it chooses to?

A: It is a potential when the vehicle so chooses. However, we are herein dealing with the other one-third, approximately, which is yet in the physical dimension of the physical realm, as it were. It is this physical cellular vibration which seeks to pull down, as it were, and slow down the frequencies which are generated from above, as it were.

E: I want more information on the symbolism and the use of the "golden key" and the "pearl."

A: The "golden key" symbolizes the gift—the ability to unlock the human mind, as it were, the total content of all that exists in the realm of the human mind.

E: If this is a gift, how can this vehicle best use this gift? Should she do this in relation to helping other people understand themselves?

A: That is indeed a part.

E: What about the "pearl"?

A: The pearl symbolizes the wisdom that is obtained when the key is applied. The pearl symbolizes the wisdom of the ages, as it were.

E: Is there anything else the vehicle needs to know about the key or the pearl?

A: Yes. It must be remembered that this vehicle must apply this upon itself as well.

E: Yes.

A: For it cannot escape the inner knowingness by helping others discover more of themselves. There is a balance to be achieved in both helping oneself and helping others.

E: That's very true. You always learn more about yourself when helping other people. All right, take another deep breath. We're going to have this vehicle go into the helix and find out how to handle the physical body in the most beneficial way to this vehicle. Going directly to the helix. Going directly in, being safe, but getting into it, getting in contact, finding out what you need to know from this helix.

A: I see an image. At first I was going through different things that looked like Light forms all over the place. All I see now is an image of a huge ball of bright white Light over here, just above and to the side. It has a cord or something on it, a connection, a wisp of Light connected to a smaller ball of Light, which is just outside of me over here. It's much smaller and almost like it's trying, something's trying, to figure out (chuckles) how do the three come together—the physical body here and the huge Light here and the smaller Light there.

E: What do these Lights symbolize?

A: The Mother, Father, Son aspect of that which we term the Holy Trinity.

E: How can this vehicle utilize that information to help her in the physical body?

A: (In a whisper) Take me to a higher level.

E: Okay. We'll count to five, and we're going to a higher level. Going into the actual Father, Mother, Son Trinity aspect, which is the highest that anyone can conceive of. When I count up to five, get into the God aspect. One, two, three, going higher, four, higher and higher, and five.

A: I don't understand. It's like that drawing in one of the books on aliens. The one book where the woman saw him come through the door of the farmhouse. There's like hundreds and hundreds coming out of it, like one right behind the other, like a tunnel or succession. They're just duplicates and they're all identical. And then the Light. When this has occurred, as these forms step out and form this type of movement, the Light steps in.

E: The Light steps in? And is it pure white Light? Is it total Light?

A: It's the white I've seen once or twice before.

E: What is your feeling about that Light?

A: I'm afraid. (chuckles) I don't know who the "I" is that's afraid.

E: All right. Another deep breath and let's find out who the "I" is that's afraid and then we'll know also why it should be afraid of the white Light. Counting to three: one, two, three. Who is the "I"?

A: The "I" is the remnant of the cellular memory which seeks to hold on, yet identify with that which it has created—generated—my memory block, as it were, which will be removed and be non-existent in the presence of the full consciousness of Light. There is a deep-seated fear that the physical vehicle will not survive the so-called transition, and until this fear has been removed, a full transition cannot indeed occur.

E: I want to speak to that fear. If, in fact, the body were not to survive, this vehicle knows very well it is only a body. If the spirit were removed from the body, the spirit could go on to higher dimensions. The vehicle knows that very well. And so, with this risk of letting that happen, this block can begin to dissolve. Why is the vehicle wanting to hold on so strongly to the physical body?

A: Because in the prior attempts of this consciousness merging with a human vessel, it was seen that the vessel was immediately terminated, as it was in a prior vehicle's Soul Exchange situation.

E: And that was prior to this particular experience with this vehicle?

A: Yes. It is the memory of that lifetime which has been transmitted and transferred to this vehicle.

E: I'd like to know a time period when that happened.

A: During the time of the being you term Christ.

E: We're not going to go into that right now, but I want to address that fear again because that was a long time ago, when the vibrations of the Earth and human consciousness were very, very dense. This vehicle must realize that the vibrations of Mother Earth have accelerated, and all of the physical bodies that are of the higher levels here on planet Earth also have the ability to accelerate further. It is not just this one vehicle called Athor.

Earth is a unique experiment, but it is possible that all, to some degree, are beginning to experience this. By letting this happen and letting go of that experience many hundreds of years ago, knowing that the situation with the Aquarian Age is extremely different, this vehicle can let go of that fear. I want this vehicle to go down deeper and deeper to release that from its body, this fear of instant extermination. Going downward, five to one. Five, four, three, deep subconscious level, two, one, flooding the body. Having the body divided into quadrants, we will flood each one with all the higher vibratory frequencies.

We give thanks for this session today to the Most High. And when I count to five . . .

A: (Athor is not ready to end the session. She begins to describe a free flow of images she is seeing.) Some special effects from that movie... whatever...a tunnel of boxes. . .

E: Okay. Breathe in deeply and continue that experience.

A: I can't judge it, as I have no reference points or understanding for what I see. I'm trying to alter it because I don't understand. I guess I'll just do a free-flow thing.

E: Yes, many of these things you don't understand to begin with.

A: It's like a womb-type situation. One tunnel of Light stacked with whatever and there's some kind of fetus floating freely in some kind of a sack, it looks like. The fetus, I don't understand this, it's like when I was regressed one time and suddenly my skin, well, this is what's happening to the fetus in the sack-like encasing. It's like something's popping out of it, inside the casing, and it looks like it's really bizarre stuff. It's a brown ... before everything was kind of like, milky ... milky to a more white side, kind of a white white. Now it's got another color, this thing inside this sack. Oh, it's a round ball and it's hard. Ow! Ow! My eyes are being turned inward. Ow! It's like somebody's pulling my eyes way back up. Ow! My eyeballs! Ow! (Her body is writhing with pain.)

E: All right. Now, I want you to get into that enough to know what it's all about.

A: Ow! My eyes! Ow!

E: What's happening with your eyes?

A: (gasping laughter) It's crazy! It feels like someone turned my eyeballs right around! Ow! Ow!

E: Do you want to experience the connection?

A: Yeah. This is weird!

E: Okay. There's a reason for this. Get into the experience and see what happens next.

A: I'm getting hot. It has something to do with the helix. It's crazy! Oh, gosh!

E: Stay with it.

A: I'm with it, but there's a part of me that's totally dark out here. It's like, what the hell?

E: Remember, it's not really happening. It's simply in your subconscious mind, and that's where it is.

A: It's a memory of something.

E: It's a memory, yes.

A: Ball is bumpy and just starting to tear apart on the outside. A golden— I don't understand any of this.

E: Just what are you experiencing?

A: I hear a lute, like a harp or something. I don't do well with my own symbolism. I see a Celestial realm.

E: I'd like to find out if this experience of the fetus and the round ball and the popping out was back during the time of Christ, when there was this transferred energy and it failed. Now you're in the Celestial realm. See if that is part of this experience. Is there anything from that experience you need to know right now, aside from the sadness?

A: Yes. An understanding of the link between my world and yours.

E: Can you give me some information to help with that understanding?

A: We have tried for eons to merge, to blend our world and yours. We have not heretofore succeeded in fully penetrating the physical shell and vivifying it fully with the Divine Essence. All those upon this plane who sought the Divinity in fullness could only reach it when leaving the physical vessel. We are attempting to bring about such a bonding that the physical vessel will be transfigured and yet maintain an existence in a form.

E: So it is extremely important to have this experiment succeed this time.

A: Yes.

E: I would like to ask a personal question. Have my vibrations been raised considerably through my contact with Rose?

A: There has been an acceleration of your previous vibratory frequency. However, it is noted that the frequencies of planet Earth are in great change. So thus, you see, you are influenced both by that which is occurring in and beyond the planet Earth, right in the outer stratosphere, and by that which is occurring in your smaller, as it were, environment in your more immediate connections and contacts with auric frequencies. Each and every one of them impinges upon the other.

Other personal questions were asked not relevant to the therapy; then the session ended.

In the conscious state, Athor explained that she attempted to incarnate in a fetus during the time of Christ but the Athor vibrations were too high and the fetus exploded. This experience was clarified in the next session. This time, when Athor incarnated into the Rose body, only one-third of the vibrations entered the body. Another third of this energy was transmitted when she was "out of the body" for six hours while lying on her college dormitory bed. The consciousness has a great fear of destroying the present body if the remaining one-third of vibratory energy is infused into the body.

Apparently, this is an experiment to determine if a physical vehicle can be infused with the Divine Essence, yet maintain an existence on Earth in a human form. (As I have had further experience with these "New Beings," I have learned that many of these experiments with Earth bodies have ended in failure. The bodies simply die. They commit suicide because of misunderstanding what is happening to them, or they are committed to mental institutions and, if released, are so heavily medicated with anti-psychotic types of drugs that they never realize their full potential. Athor is just one of these experiments.)

It became clear later in the therapy that Athor was a body of Light on Sirius, which is one of her main difficulties. Never having had a physical body before, she has great impatience with the body, since it is out of sync with her mental vibrations. This session was particularly interesting from a research point of view because it gave much information about the Soul Exchange phenomenon.

It is beginning to be apparent that this particular Athor Soul Exchange experiment is all about energy and vibrations. Athor does not see auras, but she feels them. She also "feels" the energy of books she reads. She reacts to other people on an energy level. How does their energy relate to hers? I observed later that, after Athor had completed a Soul Reading for clients, she would hug them for what seemed to me to be a very long time. I learned that she was feeling their energy. Only one client ever commented on this long hug. This particular woman asked me later what Athor did to people when she hugged them. She said that although she had slept well, she was completely unable to get out of bed the next day. She felt as if she had been drugged.

I noticed that working with Athor was a huge drain on my energy. I often felt as if I needed a long nap. There is a metaphysical concept that some people are "psychic vampires" who feed on other people's energy. Athor and I discussed her effect on me and wondered if this could be what was happening when I worked with her. We both were puzzled over this and it upset Athor when I told her about it. It was important for her to know this, however.

We needed to understand this phenomenon, particularly since vibration and energy issues seemed to be an important aspect of much of the Athor material. I now believe that the Athor energy is so high that it literally burns into the denser energy of Earth people, thinning it out, thereby allowing our vibrations to go higher. In any event, coming in contact with Athor seems to accelerate our vibrations, bringing us into a higher vibratory rate and preparing us to move into fourth density. At least this is my best explanation for the "energy issue."

I asked Athor to give her input after she read this. It is much more technical than mine. The following was written in ten minutes in a fully conscious state:

The vibratory frequencies of the Athor energy move into a person's auric field to their "essence" or "soul," stimulating that core to awaken. As the "soul body" begins vibrating and activating the lower bodies or "vehicles," the increased frequency or rate of vibration of the subatomic particles within these vehicles causes a "quickening" of all etheric and other matter which comprises the various vehicles. This quickening creates a rotational force field that repels any matter vibrating at a slower rate of speed.

As this slower matter (blocks, negativities, etc.) is repelled from the innermost vehicles outward, the person may experience some mental, emotional, or physical reactions, depending on the type of matter brought forward by the increased vibrational frequency of the soul and other vehicles.

It is somewhat akin to the action of a pebble thrown into a still pool of water. The force field generated by that pebble creates rippling circles and waves of water around it. This is very similar to the energy exchange which occurs when I hug a client or a friend and allow this energy to move through me and them. A "quick" or "bear hug" does not allow the energy to flow in this way. A certain "tuning" is necessary for me to allow this energy to flow and this takes a few seconds of focusing on my part while I am hugging someone. The same is accomplished (in slightly different fashion) by anyone who, while hugging another, opens up to the highest essence of love, or the God Force, and prays or wills it to the one being so touched.

"Dear God, help me understand. Christ, help me! I don't understand. How I want to be with God! I don't want any intermediaries. I don't want any illusions. I wish to find God. I wish to know God. I wish to be one with God. I wish this body to be healed or transformed to a higher frequency, whichever is necessary. I want to be with God."

— *Athor, July 16, 1989*

Chapter 13

Christ Consciousness

A fter this last session, Athor thought that she needed to know more about her connection with Christ. We had one session on July 11 that channeled the "Christ Spirit" through Athor. It dealt mainly with concepts related to "Light" since we had learned that Athor was a being of Light on Sirius. Although the content was quite interesting, I have not included the transcript of that session here because it really did little to further the therapy process. However, that session led into the following session, held shortly afterward on July 15. This proved to be a deeply emotional experience for Athor.

Hypnosis Session, July 15, 1989

A: I keep seeing this same image. It's not going away. The marionette— it's being shown in front of me.

E: Do you want to pursue that now?

A: We're going to have to, I guess. It's not going away.

E: All right. Just keep on with it, then. Tell me about the marionette.

A: It's just—it's wood, and it's just standing in front of me, and a string is pulled, and it moves this way, and the string is pulled and moves that way. And now I need to ask what this means.

E: All right. I'll count backwards to go in to get the meaning of this. Three, two, one. What is the meaning of the strings, of the marionette?

A: This is an image to indicate to this entity that state and condition of the human form. That it is indeed as a puppet, pulled by the strings of un-consciousness, of fate, as it were. It is indicated that this being is to take the control of these strings and to utilize it as it desires and not allow other forces to move it as they will. The being is coming into a realiza-tion of who in truth it is and, with the increased conscious awareness of this identification, the strings will indeed be controlled exclusively by the consciousness of this one.

E: Is there anything further that I need to know about this before we move on?

A: The awareness is coming. There is knowledge of that fact. The power, the peace, and the joy through the peace is imminent.

E: All right. Today we would like to try again to get in touch with the Christ Spirit coming through Athor.

A: One moment. Please proceed.

E: (I do a deepening process to go to a higher state of consciousness.) Are we in touch with the Christ Consciousness?

A: You are. (Athor is now channeling the Christ Consciousness.)

E: We would like to first of all get more information, going back to the last experience we had in talking with you, where Athor's body experienced tremendous sadness over your crucifixion, your experience here on Earth. And we would like for you to give further insight into why this had such a profound effect on Athor and her body.

A: This being experienced the sadness which it remembered from the time wherein we were both spirits, souls, before the time of my coming to this plane. As spirits, we spent much time, although there is no time in that realm, together, as it were, doing the work of the Father on planes and dimensions of which you have but little knowledge. At the time wherein my spirit infused into the Earth plane, this one wished to accompany me to help in the task at hand. It is seen that this one did split off and in its desire to accompany me, infused a very small part of itself into the human realm at the time that I embodied the form of Jesus.

It did not understand that it was to wait to see the work that had been done to gain an overview, as it were, of what yet remained to be completed on this plane. The sadness came from that identification in splitting off itself through indeed a very small part of itself. (Athor, apparently needing to deal with deep emotional issues, reverts back to her own consciousness.) Still something here, something missing here. (whispers) I want to trace the sadness to the original source.

E: You want to trace the sadness to the original source?

A: I must re-experience the sadness. It is seen—yes, it is that experience. The experience of incarnating in the fetus was my decision, was my choice, brought about because I wished to be of assistance to my brother.

E: Are you speaking now as Athor?

A: I am Athor.

E: Okay.

A: It was an act motivated by love and attachment to the Christ; thus, it was not in the flow of the grand scheme, so to speak. This being gathered unto itself a misunderstanding and a misidentification. It identified with the small part of itself which it had brought down upon this plane.

E: What role did Athor particularly play in this incarnation during the time of Christ?

A: We see again this was the attempt to join a fetus in an incarnation wherein the being exploded the physical vehicles. This was seen by the being as an act of selfishness, for it wished to follow the Christ into the physical dimension for the reason of wanting to be near and with and experience along with my brother.

E: I would like to clarify this now. You, Athor, attempted to come into a physical form and as a result of that, the body of the fetus and the mother exploded. Before we leave that, is the mother that you entered anyone that Athor knows in this present lifetime?

A: Yes.

E: Could you identify that person?

A: It is the one who presently is Rose's physical mother.

E: Therefore, Athor, entering a being born to this physical mother in this particular lifetime, came back to pay off the karma of doing that to her in the past life, is that correct?

A: Yes.

E: Because Rose would not have otherwise chosen this kind of mother.

A: Yes. And what a payoff it was, indeed!

E: Yes. I would like to ask some more questions about this now. Since you and Christ were both from a similar dimension, how was the Christ able to come into a human fetus which, according to the Biblical story, he did without exploding the mother, Mary?

A: You see, the soul's entry into the Earth plane at that time was one which was fully agreed upon—which was fully sanctioned by all concerned. It was a most timely event, you might say. My attempt was not sanctioned. It was an act of self-will, and thus the karma encountered had to be repaid, as it were, upon the Earth plane. The vehicle, this physical vehicle at this time, is encountering the last throes of that self-will. It has both judged and condemned itself for this act.

E: Since it would seem that the being has already paid very dearly for this by being born to this mother in this lifetime, number one, and also having had all of the physical problems that she has had, what is left for her to do to overcome this karma? What should she do to clear all of this up? Whom can she ask to forgive her?

A: Herself. Her own being that is in and of God always. Yet it has seen Christ the spirit, the soul of Christ, leave the spiritual realm. This, Athor misunderstood. How can there be sadness there? The sadness you experience, it comes yet from the memory of your illusion of division. What you saw as a moving away, as a leaving of your brother spirit and kindred soul, was but an expansion of growth for that one you term Christ. What you could not see was that, in his leaving in that form, he achieved a much greater form. And this you have feared. This you have seen as the separation and this you will retrace until you come to see me. (This would appear to be a conversation between Athor and the Council of Sirius.) I need to see. I need to see my people.

E: See if you can do that right now.

A: I hear that all are indeed my people. But in this act of splitting off a small part to try to incarnate through a physical form, I fell in the veil of illusion and thus could not see that even here those upon your plane are truly no different. And I identified with form and saw that to be so different. The nature of the divine is such that it propagates itself. Did you think for one moment that because your Christ left that form (emotionally) that he was no more? (This, again, is a conversation between Athor and the Beings of Sirius.)

E: Let go of all of the emotion. Let go of the feelings of sadness you are expressing.

A: What have I done? What have I done?

E: And you have had similar feelings in this lifetime down here that you have been deserted by the Christ. Is that part of this? And you're just beginning to realize—

A: Not this! I deserted!

E: You deserted. But in essence you really didn't. You were trying to follow him.

A: Yes. It takes some unraveling. There's more. Much more I cannot yet see. I feel emotion. I cannot quite see the very root cause.

E: I think that is enough for today. We can get to the root cause later. Athor may even get to the root cause on her own. But this is enough for the vehicle today.

A: This place, if you wish to call it, where I was with the Christ, the spirit as a spirit, as an individualized spirit, was in the Celestial realm. And the misunderstanding, which initially helped bring but a small part of me here, originated on that plane. The Celestial plane is of a very, very fine, fine density. And yet the beings therein also have free will.

E: I see, and you were exercising your free will when you did this, coming down here as the result of your own decision.

A: Yes. It was the intensity of that part that split off that exploded the physical vehicle, because that part identified with form. It saw the Christ as leaving when, in truth, he was evolving and changing, as all must change, yea, even on the Celestial. Growth, change is not limited to the denser forms and, in truth, it is seen that on all levels, up into the Godhead, as it were, there is yet the possibility of creating one's own reality. So there is truly none greater nor less. There is only a difference in form which is taken to—what's the word?—to manifest the realization, the understanding. So now I have to go back and spend some time there and find out what occurred exactly.

E: Now, in this present incarnation, this was planned, this was an agreement with the soul of Rose.

A: Yes.

E: So this is a different situation?

A: Yes.

E: And was this planned with the permission of the Christ?

A: Yes.

E: All right. Can we move again up to the Christ Spirit to ask more about the adjustments, since this seems to be a karmic thing now, which we were not clear on before? Again, let's see if the Christ Spirit can give any more information to Athor on these adjustments and what, if anything, she can be doing to help the process.

A: (channeling Christ Spirit again) As you can see, I have not left, nor have you abandoned me. For I am within thee and thou art within me. You will soon recognize this. And your suffering will be as naught. I AM.

E: All right. Is there any final word from either Athor or Christ before we stop the session today?

A: Yes. Many beings do not realize what a grand and glorious place this planet Earth can be. They do not realize that it is not simply a school for those who have not yet learned, but a most marvelous testing ground for the souls and beings, indeed, of every level and plane, verily unto the Godhead itself. Do not look upon yourselves as limited creatures, as limited beings. For you are all the same. You are all dancing lights in the infinite firmament of God. Each one of you twinkles and radiates as the stars in the heavens do. Those of you who suffer here and wish perhaps that you were elsewhere, look out upon the night sky, look out upon the twinkling stars up in the Father's heaven, and know that that is indeed what you all are. You are there as well as here. And indeed you are everywhere.

E: Thank you. We give our great thanks and appreciation for the information and for the messages that have come through today. When I count to five, let Rose come back into this body, grounded on this Earth, realizing that this is a testing ground. This is a marvelous opportunity to meet these tests. Being perfectly grounded, being optimistic and feeling very refreshed and energetic. One, two, three, four, five.

I do not know if Athor was indeed channeling the Christ Spirit, but I recall participating in these last two sessions with a feeling of great reverence and awe. This is a confusing transcript to read because several times Athor switched back and forth from Athor's words to those of the Christ Consciousness and the Council of Sirius. I especially related to the statement at the end: "You are all dancing lights in the infinite firmament of God." Dancing lights described my vision in the sky perfectly!

[We discovered in 1993 that the Egyptian Goddess, Hathor, was another aspect of the Athor soul. The following are excerpts paraphrased from a very long discourse regarding the early years of the Earth, channeled from Hathor through Athor.]

"When the Hathor-Athor soul was formed, we would say in your time frame, it was about five billion years ago. The Hathor energy came to Earth approximately three million years ago. When she touched down here on Earth, she would become physicalized so that people could see her. She first appeared in the Mesopotamia region. This was after the so-called "Garden of Eden." By then, there had been many experimental stations set up on the surface of the planet, and many, many beings were transported from other systems. They were "cloned" elsewhere and then transported and dropped off here in different parts of this planet. In a sense, a great darkness had descended on the surface of the planet with these various experimental modes going on, and this planet was a "dumping ground." It was similar to the English taking their prisoners to Australia in the past.

"Many groups used substances found on the planet itself to experiment with and try to create a different type of life-form. There were at least thirty to forty different groups that all experimented and dumped their offspring down here. There was basically a free-for-all which was definitely not the intention of the Beings who brought the Matrix of the planet into existence.

"The Earth itself was in a different position to the Sun. There were asteroid belts and cosmic dust belts about the surface of the planet, and it had a different gaseous structure in the atmosphere. So the Beings of that time were very rudimentary, because how else could they survive in such types of atmosphere?"

Chapter 14

Karma Explained

Much further clarification regarding the Athor story continued to occur at intervals through the rest of 1989 up until the beginning of 1992. At one point in late 1989, Athor came down with a 105 degree fever and once again she had an out-of-body experience and almost left the planet. The health problems continued. Many times Athor was in the depths of depression as the result of her disease. I finally concluded that there was no therapy I could do with her that would "cure" the Environmental Illness.

She was able to continue with Soul Readings for my clients on her good days, and this seemed desireable for her survival because she needed to use her psychic gifts. There were, however, three additional hypnosis sessions which seemed to produce substantial clarification and release at a cellular level regarding the root causes of the illness. I can only speculate on why this information did not come through earlier but all along there seemed to be a predetermined timetable for certain information to surface.

Hypnosis Session, December 3, 1991

A: Everything is dark all around, but there's this beam of Light.

E: Follow the beam of Light.

A: It ends up in a sun. It emits all these other little balls of Light that explode from it. I see a darkness and an explosion—looks like meteorites—dense objects in space. There is a seed that is on the face of a planet which begins to sprout, with which you, on this plane, are not familiar; it has a consciousness which is not known to the consciousness of those on this planet Earth. This plant propagates and produces other forms. It is not a physical dimension, close to the Earth but not quite. Propagation does not require two sexes of the species. The beings are androgynous. This is what we see as the first form of the Rose soul.

Next I see an animal-type form, different from Earth animals in consciousness, but not like something from the Angelic Kingdom. It appears to be a cross between a jackal and hyena and dog, if you can picture all three combined.

It is difficult to trace a form's roots unless it is in a body or on an astral plane. It has erased its pattern into the vast sea of consciousness. (Rose, of course, is no longer in a body.) Next is a humanoid form. It appears to be a warrior of some type—like a human. This is really hard. I see a Cro-Magnon-type man, then a warrior about five hundred B.C., and there's a very strong-looking physique in both of these pictures. This is Earth. It is very difficult to trace Rose. It chose to come to Earth because there was a limitation to consciousness it could not achieve on the other planet. The being was desirous of having further experiences.

E: Trace the past lives, which seem to be important. How many Earth lives did Rose experience?

A: She has had three hundred cycles on Earth. The being took a long, laborious path. It started from the densest level and gradually worked its way up through its final liberation from the cycles of rebirth. In between these cycles, the being had cycles where it was educated on Alpha Centauri and one or two other systems as well.

It was on one of these systems that the connection was made between the one called Rose and the Athor soul essence. The actual linkup regarding the physical exchange, which was to occur much later, occurred at the time of the Crusades, but there had been the initial meeting elsewhere first.

The being had reached the point in its evolution where it called out for the higher forces, constantly it seemed. Yet it had not fulfilled its karmic responsibilities. It was in an in-between cycle of the Earth cycles. It had a very difficult life in its prior cycle and it came to Athor through a healing place.

It was here we became acquainted as individual soul essences—one to another. It is kind of like this aspect of the Athor soul now was helping the Rose soul. It was, symbolically, like it had come to a hospital. It was a healing process and in the exchange the plan was formulated, as we had need of achieving entry to this planet and had no other means or understanding of how to go about it, unless there was a linkup made which would gradually result in a blending of the energies on different levels.

This is very difficult to describe. It was not a fusion; we are talking about eons of time. This took a very long period of time. Athor chose the particular entity Rose because it had developed a sense of compassion toward it as an individualized soul. The Athor soul was aware of the fact that the Rose soul would continue to have a very difficult path of evolution, but we could not interfere. We could only help heal during the interim periods, when it chose to leave the Earth plane.

E: Did the Athor soul continue to monitor the Rose soul?

A: Somewhat. This aspect of the Athor soul, when it was not engaged otherwise but monitoring in the terms you perceive, the duration of time you perceive, no. There was a continual connection but not in an Earthly sense—very similar to the connection between the Athor soul and that of the physical mother of Rose. This soul will always be connected with us until it has achieved its final liberation. In that way it was monitored, but not in Earth terms (Athor's Earth mother had died in late 1991 after a lengthy period in a comatose state).

E: Scan the lifetimes of Rose prior to the exchange.

A: Rose came into this cycle with a great feeling of not quite hopelessness but a feeling of great fatigue, of wishing to be done, to be finished, of feeling that ... a certain sense of failure, a sense of not fulfilling itself, for it had not yet reached enlightenment. The being itself was aware spiritually that it had had many rounds here, so to speak. It was tired out. It was on the verge of giving up but not in a positive manner.

Here again, this was a similar healing which occurred when we first met it in the in-between states. The soul was again in need of spiritual sustenance or healing. The soul reached a certain level of awareness but it did not wish to remain on the Earth. There is a feeling of guilt in Rose as well as in this aspect of the Athor soul. Guilt of the Rose soul was the result of cycles upon this plane when it had made certain promises, then it changed its mind. This changing of its mind impacted upon many individuals in many cycles. The being incorrectly blamed itself; it took on the responsibility of the guilt and thus set a whole new cycle of lifetimes where, in the past five to ten cycles, it took on all of the ills and the ailments.

It would seem to be a bit masochistic but it was more complicated because it involved its spiritual development. Because of all this suffering, it wished to alleviate the suffering. It took on all the ills of its followers and others. It could not tolerate suffering. In the cellular memory, this memory is still present. This being, Athor, has gone through much distress because of this cellular memory, which yet remains intact in the body itself.

E: Is it possible to eliminate this suffering?

A: All is possible. It is a matter of the proper alignment, if you will.

E: What is Rose's connection with Alpha Centauri?

A: The beings that vibrate on Alpha Centauri are intimately connected with what would be called the root race of Earth. The initial first differentiation of the soul Rose was on Alpha Centauri. It seems that the root race of the planet Earth was perhaps populated by Alpha Centaurians, who migrated to this planetary sphere.

E: This root race was known as the Adamic race?

A: Yes. There have been many changes which have taken place, and adaptations, but they did not retain their original form, as there was much experimentation which took place here. The Spiritual Matrix was the original blueprint, but in order to create this blueprint, the energies of the cosmic scale had to be gathered and realigned in that configuration. Once the configuration had been produced, then there were offshoots from that that were almost self-perpetuated. It was like a chain reaction. The beings of the root race were an offshoot of that original blueprint. This Spiritual Matrix was not simply limited to the human race, but it was indeed created for planet Earth.

E: It would seem that Athor has some deep seated guilt in connection with planet Earth.

A: There is a feeling of great responsibility.

E: What really went wrong with the experiment?

A: I don't see or feel anything to that question. (It was not until 1995 that information came through Athor regarding what went wrong. This information has been published in our newsletter.)

E: Now go to the memory in the body of being in the womb.

A: (long silence) It is a memory in the body, but not my memory.

E: Direct the being to enter the cellular matrix of this physical body. Now begin the birth process.

A: (Much writhing around and discomfort,) It is very dark. (deep sigh) It is very fast (sighing). The noise is getting louder. There is something happening that I don't want to explore. The body is turning inside the womb. The pounding of the heart is very loud—gurgling and rushing noises. This is difficult because it is frozen at this state of this pounding.

E: Do you still sense you are in the womb?

A: The pressure...ohhh...aawww. Pressure—my head...ummm...heavy breathing. It is like an earthquake. And the walls are starting to move. When they move it hurts, it hurts. It hurts! It's like a sucking motion... ohh...ohhh...sucking, and the body is turning...ohhh...and it's like a vacuum, squeezing and sucking on the body...Mmm. The head feels like it is in a vise...aw...ohh. My back is all scrunched up...the lower back...ohhh. The head is being yanked out and the neck is at a strange angle. The head is being pulled and yanked. It finally came out. Ohh...mmm...the pain is slowly subsiding somewhat...but now the neck ...there's a feeling of suffocation. The eyes are glued shut and this pressure goes down through the bottom—ohh…the feet…ohhh. Heavy breathing…ooh…disgust. Deep breath. It's cold. It's harsh.

They are prying my eyes open. They are glued shut. There's mucus—some kind of gluey substance. The body does not like this. The sensation…it is cold…cold…something is being done to my head. They are pushing on it, squeezing it. The pressure is different from being in a vise because the pressure comes from different directions. There are strange beings prodding and poking this body. It's not nice. This person—yuck—strange taste (now at mother's breast). This body whose womb I just came out of—it is a familiar body. Other than the body warmth, there does not appear to be any warmth. This body does not like this process. When the breast feeding is happening, it doesn't like it. There's this huge thing going in my mouth.

E: Do you swallow the milk?

A: Yes, the body needs it, but I don't like it. I feel so small next to this breast. I know I'm hungry, but I don't like it. I feel like I'm suffocating. There is a lack of sensitivity from this mother. She didn't want me because I am a representation of the guilt she feels from what she did to get me. She feels she was punished because my father did not stay with her and take on the role of a parent and husband. She feels she sinned, and I am the product of that sin. I am a daily reminder of her guilt in sinning. There is a real split because the body needs the milk, but the rest of the makeup doesn't want it. It feels like it is forced on the being.

There is a split. This cellular split has accentuated many of the physical disturbances within this body. That's where the split originated in this life, because the body needed this substance, and the being did not wish it because of the vibration and frequency so there was a split because the body was responding to the urge to survive, and drank the milk, which the whole rest of the being didn't want because it was like ingesting poison in the system. But the body needed it on a basic level, and the body did not see it as a poison. But the psyche did.

E: Relate this to the present situation with the body and food.

A: There is a definite connection. The memory has remained intact that food is a poison yet a necessity, so the body continues to ingest food, and the psyche views it as a poison and reacts accordingly.

E: What is the original origin of the body's reaction to molds and breathing? Go back to the beginning.

A: I see some children around some hay. They are crawling through the hay. One of the children is in the middle of a haystack and two older children jump off from the top of the barn onto the haystack, right on top of this small child inside the haystack, and they knock the breath out of the child. It's inside the haystack and can't move and can't breathe. It can smell the hay, the mold, the spores, but can't get out. There's a particular mold spore in the hay which is very damaging. This goes into the lungs, and the child starts having seizures, and the child dies inside the hay. It suffocated.

E: Let's find out the origin of the illness.

A: There's a great, great pain that seems to be a long, long time ago—caveman or something. He's doubled over in agony. He stumbles back to the cave. He's breathing very heavily, trying to reduce the pain. It's like a wild, living, liquid fire in the abdominal area, a fire that is burning through everything inside. He can't control it. The pain is enormous. It appears that he ate something which was highly toxic and poisonous, mushrooms or some type of fungus plant. He was hungry, and he ate something. He's in such pain that it would appear that he is dying—terrible, terrible pain. He's gone insane with pain. He's running like a madman. He falls onto some—yuck!—some vegetation and gets impaled. He jumps off a cliff and impales himself on a bush.

E: I assume that his pain followed the Rose soul in many lifetimes after that?

A: When the Soul Exchange occurred, this was the lifetime for all the karmic seeds to sprout. All remaining residual memories would thus surface through the physical vehicle. So the body of Rose carried with it all the karmic patterns of all its lifetimes into the body.

E: Was Athor aware that it would inhabit a body like this?

A: Not having had a physical form before, Athor did not have a full comprehension of that particular aspect. (laughs) That's why I'm so pissed!

We now have a much greater understanding of Athor's numerous food allergies, as well as her extreme reaction to molds. All of these problems were past-life carryovers which continued to affect the cellular make-up of the body. The next chapter finally clarifies why the Athor soul felt such profound guilt that it volunteered to come into a severely damaged body in an environment with little nurturing or support.

Chapter 15

Council of Twelve: Mission Earth

I t was not until December, 1991 that we discovered the root cause of the great sadness and emotion connected with the earlier session of Chapter 10. Finally, when Athor was able to break through many of her mental blocks and trace her origin back to the Source, we discovered, among other information that came through, that the Athor soul had not only tried to come into a fetus during the time of Christ, but it had literally forced the ejection of the Rose soul from the womb. In the process, the mother died, which we already knew, but in addition, the Rose fetus was exploded because of the high vibrations of the incoming soul of Athor. We did not know earlier that the soul in the fetus was actually the Rose soul.

In a sense, Athor really killed two people during this act, a fact which was so abhorrent to her nature that this knowledge had been blocked from her consciousness previously. Her intention, of course, was innocent. She wanted to be on Earth during the time of Jesus, with whom she had a close bond, but this so-called Soul Exchange was one of those experiments that was a disaster to all souls concerned. This was not an agreed-upon exchange. It seems that finally, during the time of the Crusades, the Rose and Athor souls agreed to balance the situation by having Athor exchange souls with Rose at a time when both again would have the same soul as a mother.

It finally made sense why Athor was willing to come into such a damaged body! This was heavy karma for a Being of Light. Most Earth beings have a history of at least one incarnation where they committed murder or some other dastardly act, but this is part of the evolutionary process of Earth. It is quite another matter for a member of the Council of Twelve on Sirius to be responsible for the death of two people.

Hypnosis Session, December 15, 1991

A: We see what would, in certain terminology, appear to be both a magnetic field and a field of Light—a pulsating central point of Light from which emanate hundreds and thousands and billions of points of Light—and the feeling…we are viewing this singular point of Light from which all these others emanate. It's almost like explosions on the sun. There are continual explosions and just continuous creation and movement and fragmentation.

We are perhaps viewing the inception of Athor, although it is some-what confusing because we are still only viewing this central point of Light from which emanate these many other balls of Light.

E: The central plane of Light?

A: The central point of Light!

E: And that central point—can you get any information on this?

A: It is stated that it is the creative force.

E: Uh-huh. Pick out the part of that Light that is the Athor soul.

A: It is not a Light. It is a moment in eternity—an ongoing process which seems to have neither beginning nor end!

E: Go to the next step after the Light separates from the Source.

A: There is a view from a planet, a point in space. It would appear to be as though it is the consciousness of a certain planet, a certain place. We are viewing space from a certain point, and there is just the conscious-ness of this specific section of the universe, of all the forms and the things that float by in space. There's just a non-personalized identity as such. It seems there is a feeling ... again, a feeling of a certain electro-magnetic field which seems to hold up a certain part of the Universe, of space. Whatever you would call it.

E: Let me be sure I'm following this. One of these points of Light went into a planet to become a consciousness of a planet. Is that correct?

A: No! It is more like the very force and substance and Matrix which holds together a certain part of the Universe. We were viewing it from a spe-cific point, but then it became the electromagnetic force field, the en-ergy behind this part of the Universe.

E: What part of the Universe are you dealing with? Is the Earth contained in that Universe?

A: Yes, although at this time there was no such physical creation as the planet Earth.

E: I'm still not exactly following this. This magnetic force was holding part of the Universe in place?

A: Yes. It provided the rotational fields for certain stars, certain planets, and certain bodies of Light. Certain formless dimensional realities were contained within this framework of energy, this grid of energy.

E: Move on to the next step of evolution now, following the Athor spark.

A: We have a more concentrated pinpointing. One moment. We see here a planet which is somewhat similar in structure or in appearance to what was viewed by this being this past weekend. (This refers to a soul origin reading done for a friend who had differentiated as a individualized soul on Venus.) But it is different. The atmosphere is not of the same substance. It also has a pristine quality to it—very beautiful, new, innocent, untainted quality. Ohh...words...it's so different from the other one, to try to describe.

E: Can you identify this planet?

A: Yes, it is what you term your Earth.

E: And what is the Athor connection with the Earth?

A: At this point? One moment.... At this point it appears that this planet Earth is almost like a holographic image in this energy field of which we spoke. And it is indeed very real within that field for, indeed, it has been created in the field, though not as yet physically. It seems to...how would I explain this? It's almost like, in very mundane terms, I have the sensation that I'm holding the Earth in this (right) hand, like a ball.

E: Move to the next step of evolvement now, of the Earth and for Athor. Before you do that, though, what is the Athor connection with the Earth that it's holding? Are there any feelings connected to this? Are there any thoughts connected to holding this Earth, as it were?

A: That place looks very similar to Venus, but the...there was a difference in feeling. Uh...you would wish to know the feeling?

E: If there is a feeling. If Athor had any feeling or thought in connection with this Earth.

A: There is no personalized identity as you perceive it at this stage of the memory. It was put into mundane terms because there were no words or capacity to express other than through those means. But this is the consciousness now as it has embodied through this vehicle making that comparison. The consciousness, as it evolved and was in existence in that field, or at that stage, did not have the type of expression or feeling of being individually personalized.

E: I understand. Let's move on now to the next step in evolution. What happened next?

A: We are watching the beings, the life forms which colonized, began upon this Earth. It would appear that at this time we are viewing what would appear to be the Devic Kingdom. This was one of the early beginnings of structuring the...perhaps stratosphere is an incorrect terminology.

E: Ask for clarification of Athor's connection with this whole process.

A: You would wish to pinpoint Athor in one small package and you have asked for the beginning of the Athor soul. You have asked for information as to the origins, the root history of the Athor soul. This is what we are presenting.

E: All right. So the Athor soul is the Earth?

A: (Sigh.) Yes, but not in the manner in which you perceive it.

E: The Earth consciousness?

A: In part.

E: All right. It would be good to clarify as much as you can. I realize how difficult it is to put it into words. But the closest you can come is that it's the Earth's consciousness, then? Is this the entire Athor soul involved in the Earth?

A: One moment, please. I keep seeing the image of this weekend.

E: Is that important? Is that connected to this? (I am getting impatient, feeling that we need to stick to the Athor soul evolvement.)

A: Yes.

E: Okay.

A: It would appear that a connection and a link for the energy has also maintained or sustained…that sphere as well.

E: Venus as well as the Earth?

A: Yes, but again we're not speaking of a humanoid, personalized type of identity.

E: Yes, okay. I understand. (I did not, really.)

A: So there would be no conscious remembrance of any feelings such as this one had this weekend, for her soul did indeed originate in that fashion upon that plane, and thus there is a big difference because it individualized on that plane and so it had feelings, sensations, etcetera, which is something that this (Athor's) soul did not have, for it was the creative force behind it which sustained or brought forth that plane and those planets, if you will. So we are now learning what it is like to be individualized upon such spheres. ("This one" referring to Athor's friend with whom she spent the weekend.)

E: All right. Now the Earth is developing with the Devic Kingdom; let it evolve from there.

A: There are many, many beings from many different systems that came upon the planet to inhabit and experiment and create a new species.

E: And those beings that come here are from other planets, other star systems?

A: Yes, many different places. Some come and go and leave samples, as it were. Others come to take, and some stay and mingle.

E: And the life forms, are they continuing to be plants or has it evolved yet into something beyond that?

A: We have the Mineral Kingdom here.

E: All right. Has it gone beyond the Devic Kingdom yet?

A: There are mists and gases, things of that sort. But there does not appear to be any solid, as you term it, physical, conscious-type of life forms yet. As a species, if you will. One moment … It is seen that the beings that stayed are utilizing some of the substances of this planet, which was not as densely physical at its inception. As far as the life forms go, it isn't like they created the species down here. They had something to do with opening up the ethers and working with the energies and all this. There was a lot of work going on. Then the Spiritual Matrix had been formed for the human species, and that was an experiment that this particular representation of the Athor soul distinctly recalls as an individualized expression.

E: How did that individualize? Tell me more about that first experience as an individualized expression.

A: I'm still looking at this planet.

E: Remember clearly the first individualized expression. It's time to remember.

A: I only see a bunch of energy. It's almost like a whirlwind, and it seems to have taken form, but there's really not much of a form. (chuckles) It's more like a ... there's a lot of energy crackling, and like almost electricity and Light shooting around it. I guess maybe it's more like a ball of Light. At first it looks like a whirlwind of energy, and then it's like a ball of Light and energy.

E: The Athor soul, the whole soul is the planet, the consciousness of the planet? (I'm trying very hard to make sense out of this.)

A: No, it is not the consciousness of the planet. It is the creative spark which formed the original Matrix of this and others as well, and thus brought it into what you would call your physical existence. And you would wish to limit it to this planet, but that is not so.

E: All right. I think I understand that. Can you clarify a little bit the choice of becoming individualized? I'm assuming that the soul itself made the choice to then start individualizing, and it did this with many different aspects of the soul. Is that correct?

A: What you have difficulty understanding, you are speaking in linear terms and in time frames that do not exist. Umm. This is an ongoing process. So it's not just that suddenly...umm.... There are all these beings that are representative, perhaps, of the Athor soul...and at one time there was not...whatever needs to be, happens here and there or anywhere within the system. To attempt to follow the entire progression would be humanly impossible, for you are viewing an energy field that encompasses an entire solar system.

E: Okay. Let's just move on then to the next step that seems to be important to remember. (I am really confused.)

A: For whom?

E: For the Athor soul that is in this body right here and now. Moving ahead from the Devic Kingdom, and then it individualizes to this whirlwind. So what else happens that we need to know, that Athor in this body needs to know?

A: If you would perhaps ask specific questions, this would be helpful.

E: (Athor always wanted specific questions, which was extremely difficult when I was having tremendous difficulty comprehending all of this information.) Can you tell anything about the Athor connection to the Animal Kingdom, as far as evolution is concerned?

A: We have only a vision ~~~~ ~

~~~~~~~~~~ ~~ ~~~ ~~~~ ~~~~ almost as though we're looking at the beings within an aquarium or a terrarium and watching and observing.

E: All right. In a sense, then, it was just observing them? I know it's not the accurate term, but something of that nature. Let's move on to when we actually have human beings here on Earth, with the soul essence in the human being. What is Athor's role at this point? Does it change from being an observer?

A: (Pause.) It's really difficult to get because it jumps back to that place at the inception of the creating—whatever this was—and then the experience of being in so many places at once and having that sensation of shock comes back.

E: View all of the early history of the Earth and find out what went wrong.

A: Well, what went, as you so quaintly put it, wrong, is that the beings were given free will. And being the quality of the Creative Force in its entirety, it could not possibly do anything different. However, the subdivisions from the Central Source of the All That Is, which fragmented off and became more individualized units, whether of human consciousness or of souls per se or of energy fields which created or held up planets or so forth—regardless of what they did as they became further and further differentiated—the issue of the free will became almost a contention.

It became a problem because it was seen from these fragmented viewpoints that many beings did not choose to use that free will in realigning harmoniously and quickly and directly back into the Source, or however you would wish to put it. And so, viewing it from the perspective of a separated condition, a differentiated consciousness from the All That Is, there was a concern amongst the beings, amongst the various energies which helped create the various species and planetary spheres and so forth.

E: Who was responsible for making the mandate or the decision that people on Earth would be given free will? Who was responsible for that decision?

A: That was a simple given, for that is the ultimate basic root seed within the All That Is!

E: Why did the Earth have more problems with this than other planets?

A: It is seen that there were many migrations from other systems and experimentations, if you will, from other systems which created a species
which was not perhaps originally intended by those of us who prepared
the Spiritual Matrix. And this influx of these various species and commingling created other species and other qualities and so forth which
were not in the Spiritual Matrix per se. Again, the free will allowed for
this commingling and mixing and so forth, but the Spiritual Matrix itself did not hold the negative elements.

E: How did Athor become involved with the Council of Twelve of Sirius?

A: The Sirius system has been in existence for a very, in your terminology,
long time. And in that span it has attracted many beings and many
consciousnesses throughout its evolution. There are some systems which
only have a singular vibratory frequency and all are joined within that,
and there is a great consensus and so forth. The Sirius system has not
had this since its inception. It, too, has evolved as other systems have
and had influxes of other beings and other energies.

And...trying to see. It appears fairly ethereal when we created the
Spiritual Matrix...umm...I don't see any particular traveling, per se.
It's almost like the Sirius system developed, became physicalized around
that plane or dimension which created the Spiritual Matrix for both the
planet and the beings upon it. So it's almost like it just evolved. And I
was there. I want to say from the beginning.

(This was really not the case. Finally, in 1994, we found that the
Athor soul originated in the Realm of the Gods. This will be discussed
in Chapter 17.)

First, there were only the inner planes and the inner realities, and as
they gradually expanded outwards, the Sirius system was developed
and created, but this was all contained within that system. I don't see
any particular individualized—if that's what you're asking for—single
unit of consciousness traveling there. No, we do not see this. Rather, it
is the evolution around the inner planes from which this being came,
which then created the Sirius system. And, having been involved on the
inner planes, the inner realities, before the system became physicalized,
as such, then it would just follow naturally. It is much like the growth of
a tree, which expands and grows outward from within a seed, a center
core.

E: I'm still wondering how Athor, being on the Council of Twelve, fits into
all of this. I just don't understand that.

A: The beings from the inner planes and the inner dimensions, from this
one memory I was able to access, wherein the Spiritual Matrix was

formed, more or less stayed together, I'd say. That's not a very correct term. So they evolved together and part of that evolvement created the Sirius system.

E: This was before the Earth was created?

A: Yes.

E: Okay.

E: After Sirius was created, then the next giant step, perhaps, in evolution for Athor was to be in a form that is more physical, I presume. Therefore, did it pick this particular member of the Council? I still don't quite get the connection.

A: The members of the Council as such do not have form, per se. However, they do on occasion transmute the substance to produce form in order to communicate with those beings within the Sirius system and other systems that require this type of expression. The form for which you asked a description, it was stated then that we are not concerned with form, but in order to humor you and others who would wish to have some representation, it was given. A description was given that is one which, again, is taken on from this substance which we are.

E: What is Athor's relationship to the other members of the Council of Twelve?

A: Many of these energies, beings, have been involved in much creative activity in many sectors of not only this galactic system but others as well, and there is a consensus of (chuckles) I guess, creativity, if you will.

E: It is said in some books here that Sirius is a technological kind of system. Is that part of the technology then, the creation of these systems? Is that part of the technology as general practice?

A: We have varying levels of beings in the Sirius system, and to say that this particular—umm—this creating and so forth is our technology for the Sirius system is incorrect, because it is something which is only held amongst the Council members. And it is not given freely, shall we say, to those who are not so predisposed to be able to properly utilize it.

So the others—the Sirians per se—uh ... yes, are indeed technologically advanced in many ways from some other systems, but this particular aspect is not shared with the population or the beings at large. This means that only the Council of Elders is involved in Creation, but the other Sirians are also technologically advanced along different levels.

E: Athor, from all we have observed, voluntarily took on this very damaged body and we assume it was because of feelings of guilt. Now, if it's totally misunderstood guilt because everything that has been said today would indicate that things were just evolving as they should, or is there some misunderstanding about this? Where has all the guilt come from? It may be guilt that's misunderstood and doesn't even exist, but simply that we take these kinds of things on. Find out what that guilt is about, even though it may be false guilt.

A: The guilt stems originally from the fact that there was not a consensus of all these beings that I have seen when we called on the energy of the Solar Logos to create the Spiritual Matrix. There was one dissenting energy and consciousness that tried to, of its own free will and choice, inhibit and stop this process. The being had never experienced dissension before because this was as individualized as it had ever become to that point, and so it didn't know any dissension, it had never personalized form, and so this was a great shock. There were only nine or ten beings there.

E: These nine or ten, what did they have in common? What was their bond? Why would there just be nine or ten making these decisions?

A: They were representatives chosen by the various systems to pool their resources, as it were, their energies, etcetera, to help bring this about, for every stage of creativity requires certain skills and knowledge and comprehension and understanding, and there were many, many factors which needed to be implanted and imprinted into this Matrix, and these varying individuals each had a contribution to make toward that end.

E: Can you give any information on why this one entity wanted to stop the process?

A: (Long pause) All I get is he did not want to lose the form, although it was very etheric.

E: By creating this Matrix, this would diffuse the form per se, and it would be split apart more?

A: Yes.

E: Okay.

A: It was like each being had a certain contribution, a certain input, a certain energy, and they all had to be combined. But it wasn't as though each being, through their individualized input, could throw it all in a pot. That's not how it worked. That energy, that input, was directed into a central, uh, chamber, if you will. The one designated who would take the next step would be, in this case, the Athor soul. It would combine that energy, then channel the Solar Logos, and in so doing would essentially, from its own essence, give birth, and in order to do that, that form would be dissipated.

E: Okay, moving ahead. See if there is anything else that needs to be explored in regard to Athor and the Earth prior to the time of Athor trying to take on a body on Earth during the time of Christ.

A: (Long pause) I hear "yes," but ... .

E: The primary focus of this has always been to see what ~~~

~~~ to this incarnation that has not surfaced before? If so, we call on the Beings of Light, the Higher Christ Consciousness, the Father-God-Creator Source, to bring forth this information through Athor's consciousness. Tell her what else she needs to explore.

A: Well, I'm seeing this image of an infant taken up by Angels and I don't know ... the first thing I got was that being when I tried to incarnate in the physical. The infant was the soul of the one named Rose.

E: It was not Athor?

A: There was another being. The mother had a soul during the time of Christ and so did the infant, and I was not, I guess, aware and I tried to enter the womb, to incarnate.

E: Meaning Athor?

A: Yes, and that was the one that this time was released in a much gentler—I mean, it was happy to go this time.

E: I'm still confused. I want to be absolutely clear. Athor wanted to incarnate?

A: At the time of Christ. And it exploded the bodies of the mother and the fetus, the energy.

E: So this infant—did you have any connection with this?

A: Yes. This infant, who was actually going to incarnate through that womb, that I more or less forcefully tried to take, was the Rose soul.

E: Oh! This was like a Soul Exchange situation, almost. The original soul that was in that womb was the Rose soul. Athor tried to enter the Rose soul to replace her?

A: Yes!

E: But Rose was happy to go?

A: No. This time. This time! They are showing me that the cycle has been completed for that soul and for my connection to that soul.

E: Oh, I see! If that process has been completed, can the body also let go of the damaged cells which originated with the Rose body?

A: If this consciousness (as Athor) chooses to manifest the transmutative capacities, yes. But because we are working with the physical here, the physical has its own timetable, and it can be transmuted only to the degree of the acceptance of the awareness.

E: What does this mean, in terms of how Athor can perceive she can heal herself? Let me put this a different way. Is it the intention of this experiment with Athor to have this body so connected with the Earth and all of the density on Earth that this whole experiment has literally been what she said from the very beginning, that the Athor consciousness has taken on all the problems of the planet, taken on all these energies and, in doing so, has created these problems for the body. Is that correct?

A: I hear "yes" and "no."

(Laughs. This kind of answer is always frustrating.)

A: (Stretches and sighs, chuckles)

E: Did Athor take on this body because of false guilt?

A: Yes.

E: Can Athor, at this particular time, release all of that false guilt? Is she willing to do that?

A: I hear "yes" but my logical mind says "how?"

E: Is the process that she is using with the white Light to be continued, and will this heal the body?

A: Eventually. They are not telling me that it's going to be easy. (sighs)

E: Will Athor be well enough to participate in some workshops in May of 1992?

A: If the ritual of Light is adhered to faithfully daily, with some variations, it is seen that, within three to six months, there will be a gradual increase in this physical body's capacities to withstand foreign energies for, as it stands now, the body is greatly weakened by the surrounding atmospheric pressures and energies, both vibrationally as well as physically. Thus, it behooves this one to daily surround itself in the living, pulsating Light in a conscious manner, for that is the only protection this being has.

E: Is there anything else that we need to know about the Athor soul for its evolvement?

A: I hear "yes."

E: Let's again call on all the Beings of Light involved in this whole experiment. Who is responsible for this experiment? Who made the decision to experiment besides the soul? Who else was involved in this experiment?

A: All I hear is the "All That Is." (laughs) Sorry, that's what I hear.

E: Is this soul a true Soul Exchange or is this a braiding of the souls of Rose and Athor? (I had just learned about the Soul Braiding phenomenon.)

A: Braiding not in the manner in which it is understood here, although there has been a deep connection due to the fact that this one thought it could take on the vehicle with which another soul was involved and had planned to incarnate. And so this soul has felt it needed to do penance, you might say, for this act which if anything

it appeared to be quite the opposite, and the soul, from the perspective from which we saw it, had intended to incarnate but the consciousness pushed it out, so to speak, in order to appropriate that vehicle, not entirely understanding the methods and so forth that went on here, having not individualized and having no lineage of physical form expression. So there was a close connection, certainly, between these two in that the responsibility which I felt, and in that sense there was a certain bonding of energies, only from that sense of responsibility and of wishing to make it right, in the sense that this is one and the same. It is an aspect. It is a spark. It is a fragment that belongs to another grouping, as it were.

However, the memories and the cellular makeup have not been transmuted because the Athor being has been confused and has not fully accepted itself. I have not accepted myself and my own destiny and beingness. This is just gradually and slowly coming together here. You know all the doubts and the conflicts and all these other things that are still in the memory banks that are partly mine and partly what was left in the memory banks of the other being in the cells. All that stuff is still there. And without conscious work on this, it's not going to go away. This is part of my individualized process.

There is another aspect to learning what this individualized learning is down here. Because everyone has to undergo this here. Maybe not with another being, but they certainly have to deal with their own past-life cycles and subconscious tendencies that are buried deep within, etcetera. So I'm doing nothing different from others merely because I need to study this, to understand this, and to get on with it.

E: Are you being studied constantly?

A: Yes.

E: You are linked up with the Council?

A: Yes, and with others.

E: They are monitoring what you do?

A: Yes. But I certainly have been given free choice.

E: I again ask from the Highest Sources to bring forth any more information and we will conclude after that. Is there any additional information that is really important to know now?

A: (Long pause) This pamphlet which speaks of the 11:11 is correct in many respects. However, it is indicated that the influx of energy that is due to come is more in the shape of a V form and the emphasis upon energy transmission should be focused upon the bottom of this V, for that is the fulcrum point between these two beams of Light that will come through the surface of this planet, and then the process will widen the gateway, for these energies can only be brought through in small and increasing increments.

As the vibrational frequencies of the beings upon this plane are increased, this in turn creates a resonating capacity, a magnetic attractive capacity for this energy to come forth. But it is seen that the energy will come forth in a bipolar fashion. One will come forth from the realms of Light, and one will come forth from the other.

E: From the negative?

A: Yes. And it is where the two merge down upon the Earth that the full extent of the prayers, the meditations, the sending of Light should be concentrated. For it is here where the blending will occur. For the transmutation is not all that is connected and concerned here. We are dealing here with the transmutation of forces of energy, not simply of consciousness for a race or a group of beings. We are dealing with the transmutation of forces and to transmute the forces of the negative into Light requires a blending, a surrounding if you will, of the negative into the Light. And with this blending the darkness cannot exist.

E: Thank you. We ask that Athor be given information to give to the group on January eleventh, which will be helpful to the group. (I held a large group event on January 11, 1992 to assist in opening a doorway to a higher dimension.)

Although there had been many references at various times regarding the Council of Elders on Sirius, I had found it quite difficult to accept the concept of Athor actually being an embodiment of an aspect of one of these Elders. This apparently was even more difficult for Athor to accept, although from an early age she had sensed that she had much inherent power. She had always been afraid of this power.

She told me once of an incident where she was driving at night and ran over a raccoon. When she stopped the car to go over and look at the animal, it was obvious that it was badly injured and, in fact, appeared to be quite dead. She decided to test her power, since she felt there was nothing to lose. She directed Light toward the raccoon, and in a few moments it stood up, circled three times, and moved with such grace that it seemed to float above the ground as it slowly walked into the woods.

This experience was frightening to Athor. Of course, at that time she still thought she was Rose and this "power" made no sense to her. Since I have known Rose-Athor, she has had a real problem dealing with anyone she feels is misusing power.

In our discussion after her very first ~~~~~~~~~~~~~~~~~~~~~

~~not mean~~ everyday-type mistakes, which she made frequently, but rather a "mortal mistake." It would seem now that this deep-seated fear originated from the time when she misused her power by attempting to incarnate into a fetus without permission, from the one she was trying to enter (the mother), the soul she was attempting to displace (the Rose soul), or the Council of Elders. This was a supreme misuse of power.

After this last regression, both Athor and I finally concluded that she indeed must have come to Earth directly from an existence on Sirius. And as unbelievable as it seems, I am convinced Athor is an aspect of one of the Beings of Light on the Council of Elders.

Much of this transcript was quite confusing to me. Athor explained later that she was involved in creating the Matrix of Earth but she was also involved in creating many other planets. One of the beings did not agree to the plan. Apparently, the consensus was to continue with the experiment and Athor was the one elected to send out the first beam of Light directed toward the creation of the Matrix of Earth. Consequently, she feels a particularly heavy responsibility for the Earth.

The Earth experiment has not turned out as planned. According to later information, Athor states that the Garden of Eden, which was not totally physical but close to it, was the first experiment with beings akin to the present form of humankind. However, when these beings were given free choice (metaphorically, ate of the tree of knowledge of good and evil), the original plan began to change drastically. Therefore, I theorize that the Council made the decision to send one of its members here to Earth to investigate firsthand the results of this rather disastrous experiment. Since Athor had incurred karma through her insistence on incarnating earlier without permission, she volunteered to come to Earth to balance her karmic debt and to help straighten out the mess here on Earth. Of course, as she stated, she is just one of these Light Beings here at this time to assist Earth. It would seem, however, that she got more than she bargained for in accepting the assignment of entering a severely damaged body and an abusive family environment.

Since the initial agreement for the Soul Exchange took place during the time of the Crusades, I again theorize that Athor and the Council were able to project into the future and pick a time when there would be some possibility of success with such an exchange. Early in the history of the Earth, a person such as Athor would most likely have been hung or burned at the stake as a witch. Even now, her mission is a very dangerous one because of the extreme health problems of the Rose body. As mentioned in this session, Athor is constantly monitored by the Council in order for the members to try to comprehend the emotional traumas of Earthlings.

I thought we finally had all the answers to the puzzle of Athor's Soul Exchange, but she still insisted there was one part she did not understand. This led to one more important regression in early 1992.

"The Yeti, or Bigfoot, is a creature which exists upon your plane in the interdimensional spaces between the physical plane dimension and sub-level within it. It is incorrect to say above or below it, as such it is within it. So, thus, this being has the capacity to materialize in the physical form as well as dematerialize into a slightly finer form, which is at times invisible to the physical eyes of your people ...they are, in a sense, like a bridge, somewhat of a gateway. They are helpers, as it were, but are upon the thresholds of almost two evolutionary species, you might say. They are an in-between state of evolution."

— *Athor, February 6, 1990*

Chapter 16

Death in the Himalayas

D uring the summer of 1990 we had discovered that Rose was an archeologist in her most immediate past life. The Rose soul, a professor, was on an expedition in the Himalayas when his party of explorers was approached by a Yeti (Bigfoot). The other members of the party went into a state of panic, deserting the professor. The professor, Marcus Yasuf David Schemmel, was taken by the Yeti to a place where his body was beamed up to a spaceship, and much experimentation took place on the body. As the reader will recall, in one of the earlier transcriptions, there was mention of a being which felt that it was trapped here on Earth. At the time we had thought that this was the Rose soul, but this never made sense to Athor. Finally, we were able to clarify the "trapped entity" puzzle in early 1992.

Since the encounter with the Yeti and the ET experimentation on the body covered a number of sessions, I am condensing the story to include only the most important points. The following is Athor's attempt to describe the terror and shock of that ET encounter.

Hypnosis Session, June 12, 1990

A: It is very hard to describe the tremendous shock that being experienced, the terror and fear felt until the consciousness just shut down and shut it off. At first there was a tremendous shock to the system, and it registered sufficiently so that it was retained in the memory, in the cells of that being. And the memory was again brought forth in the cells of this body.

The purpose was to determine, as much as possible, the full extent of what would be involved in the genetic structuring and mutation of the physical form of this one Yasuf, the professor. And in particular, as it is representative of a human body, to determine the extent of the physical changes in terms of the environmental factors existing upon planet Earth, the emotional changes, and the mental changes. However, it is noted that the beings were apprised of the fact that this one, Yasuf, could only be altered in what you would term the head area, as the rest of the body would not withstand the shock.

There was a tremendous amount of shock initiated upon that being's memory banks and cellular mechanism, as well as the mental body processes. And it was seen that the experiment had to be terminated before the full physical vehicle was mutated, as it would h~~~~ sation of nhv~i~~l l:f~ ~~

~~~~ ~~~~ ~~~~ ~~at occurred within the physical ~~~ ~~~~~ vehicles of this being, Yasuf. However, as the being only remained for a period of twenty-five to thirty-five days upon this plane after this experiment, the hoped for data was not collected, as it was seen that such a procedure was too drastic and radical, and these beings, as well as others who were not immediately present, had to "go back to the drawing board" in order to determine what to do next.

A probe or tracking device had been implanted into the brain of Yasuf but, as stated, this experiment failed, since the shock was too great for Yasuf to survive.

Athor kept trying to understand the trapped entity from Alpha Centauri. She finally understood that this was definitely not the Rose soul when we received clarification in the following transcript. I was hesitant to even include this information because it sounds so much like science fiction, but as Athor has continued to give soul readings for many of my clients, we are finding that many, many people have had similar types of experiments performed by ET groups or entities. In fact, the experimentations by ETs seem to be accelerating, although most of them, we have discovered, have been more of a positive nature than the traumatic experiment on the professor.

Athor continued to feel that there was one more part of the puzzle which needed to be clarified. She had some insights into the "trapped entity from Alpha Centauri." The following transcript clarifies this issue.

Hypnosis Session, January 28, 1992

A: It is indicated there was a great deal of fear in this memory as the professor's soul body was laid on the table in this ship. There were many beings surrounding it from many systems. They were studying the energy systems and vehicles of the Yasuf Schemmel soul body in preparation for an experiment in which they hoped to join one of their species into the etheric and astral vehicles. There were many energy adjustments and incisions made, much akin to what your present-day psychic surgeons would produce.

The Rose consciousness, though somewhat unaware, yet had the rudimentary consciousness on a cellular level that this was totally foreign to its existence and to its knowledge, etcetera, so it experienced much fear and in the course of that fear, there were some molecular and hormonal changes that occurred in the body cells. With the experimentation that was going on in the body, it seemed that the body was coming close to a point of physical death, and the beings did not wish this to occur.

Not knowing the full extent of these body systems here and their level of function and activity they, in a desperate attempt, sought to infuse their own essence into this body to keep it alive and in the course of what happened, the Alpha Centauri soul essence entered the vehicles of the professor's auric bodies even though the professor's soul was still present in them.

It's almost like a warp in time because the Rose soul (the professor at that time) was aware that the exchange was going to take place between the Athor soul and the Rose soul. That was a soul knowledge and recognition and understanding. However, it did not have this soul knowledge and understanding with these beings. Thus it is seen that, as the other essence entered the vehicles, it could not enter the body because there was already a soul essence within it, so it entered the auric vehicles and sort of damaged the vehicles as a result because it could not expand to its fullest capacity, and the other one, the Yasuf soul, was also extremely restricted. And thus was the case of two souls within one bodily system, neither of them being very happy about the situation.

E: Would this be termed as a possession or a Soul Braiding?

A: It is neither. In the case of possession, the motivating factor of the possessor is negativity. The motivating factor in this experiment was one of panic and desperation, trying to keep the life force continuing on the level on which it had existed prior to this experiment.

E: So it primarily entered the body to keep it alive.

A: So then, since it was extremely experimental and was not well thought out and did not follow the known laws, etcetera, the being itself, the soul of the future Rose, was in a state of shock. It sort of retired its Light, you might say, further out into the causal body. In part, it was the mental body. Now the real terror came through the emotional bodies, wherein the Alpha Centauri soul felt trapped.

When a soul enters a vehicle through other than the incarnation process, there are a set number of rules and regulations which must be adhered to in order to effectively process this. Now these rules and regulations were not known to these beings, so they produced a hybrid-type creature that was totally lost because neither soul could fully allow its Light to shine forth and go forth into the vehicles because there was not room. The other soul had commandeered these vehicles here (pointing about one to two feet away from the physical body) and the other one had these vehicles (again pointing to an area about thr~~ ~~ feet away from the ph~~~~~~ ~ ~

~~~~~~~~ ~~ ~ᴏnsciousness.

~~~ ᴀ ᴵᴇsuit ᴏr that, when the being went into the cave and was communicating with the beings from the ship, the communication hit both beings, both souls, on different levels, and there was such a resultant jarring effect on the physical body that it simply died because this was not to be. This cannot be done, not on Earth, unless the two souls are equally matched in vibrational frequencies. Then it is possible. Then you have what is termed a Soul Braiding. If the frequency is not harmoniously matched, then this is not possible.

Two people had said, when they were looking at my auric field, they couldn't understand why some of my bodies were almost flattened, and there were all kinds of strange things going on in the bodies because of these energies still there and the lack of understanding. Sandy (a friend who is also psychic) agreed that not a lot of me was here, and I've been working for a long time to get myself here, but I don't know how to do it. I had no methods, no means because she said that the thing with my body is not my doing because she had never seen this before. She looked and looked and saw these two balls of Light. I know I didn't create this body, and that's what I wanted to do. Outside of the Soul Exchange, I didn't create the body, but this body had so many problems and so much darkness around it, it was a horrible trip.

E: When the Athor agreement was made, this was not what had been planned?

A: No. Again, here we have a similar thing like with the Spiritual Matrix. What occurred on this planet was not what we planned either, and not what we intended when the Spiritual Matrix was formed. That's why I came here, to find out what in the world went wrong and how to correct it. You know, I'm just one of the many beings here from other systems who have the same thought in mind and know that the dimensional energies are changing. So they are all down here utilizing their abilities. They have to help bring this about.

E: Is the Matrix battle between the forces of darkness and Light?

A: No. It happened before that. I finally got a message from Gehema. "When you look at a flower and the pollen is like the seed, that is like the life force that reproduces." Well, Gehema is the seed of Light. I am on the Council. I was the builder. I took that and gave it form. So that's the connection. Whenever I think of Gehema, I just go—poosh! Gehema told me, "You also have that seed within you. Look deep within. Look for me." Well, that's going to take a while on a total level like I want to. It's just the smallest beginning of what I need to do. This is the first time in my life I have absolutely no fear. I have an energy field, and finally it is mine. That's why I'm no longer afraid.

(End of hypnosis session.)

We had discovered earlier, while working with Zonatar, another client who appeared to be a Soul Exchange that, after the initial exchange of souls, the energy of the old soul in the auric bodies must be cleared out or purified. This process can take many months, or even years. The timing of this process seems to vary with each individual. In Athor's case, since she had all the effects of the trauma of both the Rose soul and this ET from Alpha Centauri locked into her emotional body, the feelings of fear and sadness continued to persist until, through regressions, she was able to finally tap into the memories of the traumas and release the emotions connected to the memories.

Athor has continued to suffer bouts of allergy attacks, but they no longer seem to be life-threatening. She finally has a sense of her real essence and a strong desire to get on with her mission of service to the Earth. I feel that one of her primary purposes is to help humans have a more in-depth understanding of the soul as related to the entire Universe through the Athor Soul Readings.

I thought we finally had all the pieces to the Athor puzzle, but as time went on, I realized that we really did not know exactly what happened to the Rose soul, and I was still somewhat confused about the role of the soul from Alpha Centauri. The following transcript clarifies these issues.

Hypnosis Session, October 6, 1992

A: The Alpha Centauri soul, at the time it exited the old vehicle (the professor) in that cycle, was caught in a time warp, an energy field that it basically drew around itself because of the occurrences that happened, because of what it did. The motive at the time it entered the auric field of the Rose body was one of trying to maintain that life force. That was seemingly a positive motive. However, the fact remains that this, in a sense, was a meddlesome type of activity, which was not so different from what the Athor essence attempted at the time of Christ.

You see, this being from the Alpha Centauri grouping was certainly at a higher level of evolution than many beings on this plane and therefore did not have the liberty—it had the free will, yes—to do this type

of thing. But given its greater level of awareness, it is not so easily—
how would you say—it doesn't get away with it quite as easily as a
being of lesser awareness, so that the lesson for the being was appropriate to its level of consciousness. And that lesson was that ~~when it ~~
~~ited the~~ ~~Va~~ ~~f/D~~

~~...~~~~...~~~~..~~~~s actions, which pro-~~
~~pelled~~ it into a type of whirlwind from which it could only be released
when it fulfilled its karmic obligations.

It had no karmic obligations until the very exact moment that it
entered the auric field of the professor. When it exited the professor
vehicle, it went into this energy state which required that it return to the
physical vehicle and exit as one soul, or one being, from one vehicle.

E: So it went into the fetus of the child, Rose?

A: Yes. The soul essence did indeed come through the vehicles. However,
the vehicles around this particular physical body were created by the
energies and karmic tendencies of the Rose soul. But the Alpha Centauri
soul essence then had to enter through these vehicles, from which, of
course, it was most, most happy to be released when the final exchange
occurred.

E: Was the Rose soul even in the body in this lifetime?

A: Not the soul itself. It is seen that, in the last incarnation of the Rose
being, the soul Light of the Rose soul was liberated. It was allowed to
go on. It was no longer required to maintain a focused connection with
the Earth plane. By that we mean, as a soul essence, it did not give its
full attention to this life cycle. However, it had created the vehicles and
these vehicles had not been fulfilled and fully transcended.

The energies of the vehicles which the Rose soul had created were
yet intact. And, yes, as is the case when a soul leaves a body, the astral
shell generally dissipates but the unresolved karma (the samskaras, the
seeds of the karmas) yet remains as energy pockets, and the soul that
returns to fulfill that karmic obligation is coming through the spheres
and then again picks up these energies. It does not pick up the exact
same astral body because that is dissipated, and certainly the etheric
bodies are completely annihilated at the time of physical death or shortly
thereafter. Some of the higher vehicles, such as the mental body and
causal body, were certainly intact and these energies had to be played
out. And, in that sense, the Rose soul still had a connection, a connecting Light to these other vehicles.

It is seen that the Alpha Centauri soul essence had to take on a full
residence (which is somewhat incorrect) but it certainly brought through
more of its essence through this vehicle in this incarnation than the

Rose soul. One ray of Light went from the Rose soul essence to the causal body of the Rose child and the Alpha Centauri essence came in as a soul essence.

When it came through, it brought through the energies which were yet remnants left from the Rose soul because these karmas had not been fulfilled. It brought in those qualities as it came through because it was determined karmically that the Alpha Centauri essence had to incarnate to fulfill that obligation, which it had created in its unconsciousness, even though, again, we state that its conscious motive was one of trying to help but for the level of its awareness and evolution this was, in a sense, inexcusable.

E: Now you said that the Rose soul was allowed to go on. Where did it go after it was liberated?

A: It went to a level within the Celestial realm where it has remained as an energy source in a formless fashion, as pure energy. It is seen it will remain in this state until such a time when the All That Is (the interpenetrating Creative Force) moves it elsewhere. So, in essence, it has become one with the Source but in a somewhat limited fashion because it is still an individualized energy unit.

E: So the All That Is could remove this energy and let it begin a new series of experimentation?

A: Yes, that is so.

This session brings up many philosophical questions with regard to the soul, but to delve into these issues is beyond the scope of this present book. Athor and I are now satisfied that we finally understand the many facets which entered into the Athor experiment.

"The Angelic Realm is the main ~~~~~~~~~ ~~~~~~~~

layers of the Celestial Kingdom, you might say. This is inadequate at best, but we do not have the words in Earth terminology to explain.

"The Celestial realm has other substrata, both beneath and within it. You see, we are not speaking of a linear formation here and so it is difficult to put into your terminology. This is not a star system, nor a dimension, but a realm. A dimension is a level of frequency wherein there is a certain series of frequencies. A dimension has seemingly more of a series of boundaries than a realm. Anything below the sixth-dimensional frequency is what we speak of here. In the first through fifth dimensions there is an element of some type of boundaries. A realm does not have so many boundaries. A realm can be composed of many dimensions and dimensional frequencies."

— Athor, October 6, 1992

Chapter 17

Conclusions

To conclude the discussion of the therapy, this chapter is a summary of the major conclusions of the "Athor Saga." Athor was one of the "Creator Beings of Light" involved in the creation of the Matrix, or blueprint of the Earth. This creation was akin to the Biblical "Garden of Eden," a beautiful, pristine dwelling place with an abundance of vegetation and all that anyone would need for a peaceful existence. When the symbolic Adam and Eve ate of the "Tree of Knowledge," they recognized good and evil or, in other words, the possibility of duality (positive and negative forces). Adam and Eve were representatives of the original species of Earth beings, the Adamic race.

The Beings of Light who created Earth allowed this knowledge of duality because this is part of the freedom of choice, a universal law. However, some planets had been destroyed and others had evolved into a higher dimension or vibration (third dimension into fifth). The beings from these other planets who had not evolved sufficiently to reincarnate on a fifth dimension planet or whose home planet was destroyed, were allowed to incarnate on Earth in order to work out their karma and continue with their evolutionary process. In addition, many beings from other planetary systems became interested in Earth and began their own genetic experiments.

Thus Earth became a great "melting pot" of this universe. This caused tremendous chaos on Earth, with these various beings with a different heritage of destruction and anger playing out the negative duality, and bizarre creatures being created. Although the various Galactic Councils had given permission for this to happen, the results were not as planned or anticipated. As a consequence of the negative forces overcoming the positive forces repeatedly throughout the history of the Earth, this planet has been a very slow learner, with relatively little progress being made over millions of years.

When the atomic bomb was exploded and additional nuclear devices began to be developed, the Galactic Councils made the decision that off-Earth beings had to become involved in the affairs of planet Earth to prevent Earth's inhabitants from destroying themselves, which in turn would have an effect on the entire solar system. Something new needed to be devised by the Councils to help planet Earth survive a nuclear holocaust and to continue evolving into a fifth-dimensional planet.

The new plan was to have thousands of "star seeds" incarnate at this time. In addition, many other experiments have been devised to develop a new, highly evolved species here on Earth to help with the transition. With enough of these kinds of Beings of the Light thi~ ~~~ ~~ ~ ~~~~~ ~~~~~~

..., ~~~~~ that the following are two kinds of experiments:

1. Beings whose primary existence has been off-Earth have incarnated on Earth at this time of transition toward the end of the twentieth century.
2. Through the Athor readings, we have discovered that some of my clients are participating in "New Being" experiments. These experiments have always been part of the plan to help with the Earth's giant leap into a new vibration, but because we are now reaching the time for Earth to shift into a higher dimensional planet, they have increased dramatically. I believe that these New Beings, along with the thousands of contacts between Earthlings and extraterrestrials, now comprise the central part of the plan to assist Earth.

In my understanding, there probably have been Soul Exchanges here on Earth for many thousands of years, always with the purpose of having humankind evolve to a higher level. However, the difference now is that the Soul Exchanges seem to involve an exchange between an Earth soul who has earned the right to return to the Light and an extraterrestrial soul, unlike earlier exchanges in which the entering soul was one who had many previous incarnations on Earth and therefore was simply a highly evolved Earth soul. The latter type of exchange may still be occurring, but I have not had any cases of this nature in my private practice.

Keeping this background of the Earth in mind, let us summarize the Athor story. Athor is an aspect of one of the Beings of Light on the Council of Twelve of the star system Sirius. These are some of the Creator Gods, for lack of better terminology. They decide what should be created, what the method of creation should be, and where in the Universes the creations should occur. The star system of Sirius was formed from the energy of the beings on the Council. These Council members originated in the realm of the Gods—a line of evolution with approximately one hundred and twelve beings whose duties are to create.

Athor was one of the beings chiefly responsible for the initial creation of the Spiritual Matrix of Earth. As such, she and the other members of the Council have been appalled at the on-going negativity prevailing on Earth. The Earth is lagging greatly behind the rest of our galaxy in terms of spiritual development. However, this has also afforded the opportunity for souls to learn lessons that cannot be learned anywhere else in this galaxy at the present time.

Be that as it may, at a soul level, Athor has felt a strong responsibility to try to help the Earth. The Council felt that the best way to assist Earth was to have one of its members take on an Earth body which would be monitored by the Council, thereby experiencing firsthand the negativity here on Earth. Athor volunteered because it was her soul's energy (spark of creation) that initiated the birth of the Earth. (This, at least, seems to be the case from the information provided in the trance sessions.)

All the members of the Council realized that this would be an extremely difficult assignment, but Athor had an additional motivation for incarnating on Earth. She had attempted an incarnation during the time of Jesus, with the hope of assisting him during a very difficult lifetime. However, at that time the Athor soul did not have the permission of the Council, which approves Soul Exchanges. Therefore, the experiment was a devastating failure. Both the baby already in the womb and the mother of the baby were killed when Athor attempted entry because the frequency of the Athor soul was too high to permit a successful entry.

This resulted in Athor incurring a strong karmic debt to the mother and fetus she destroyed through this aborted Soul Exchange. The fetus was the Rose soul, and the mother of that fetus was the present mother of the Rose soul in this lifetime. Thus, by making the exchange with the Rose soul, Athor could allow the Rose soul to leave and go to the Light, a reward the soul had earned through hundreds of lifetimes, and at the same time Athor could allow herself the experience of being the child of the mother she had destroyed in the lifetime during the time of Jesus.

This served many purposes, since this particular mother was a soul who was still in much darkness. By being with Rose-Athor in this lifetime, this soul could get some concept of the Light, but she also contributed to the experiment by providing an extremely negative, abusive childhood experience for Athor. She contributed to the allergy problem through Rose's rejection of the milk in her breasts. Although Rose knew at the subconscious level that she needed the milk to live, she hated it. This led to the body's strong rejection of food in general. With a stepfather like Karl, this kind of dysfunctional childhood was an ideal setting for the Athor soul to begin experiencing the negativity present on Earth.

One of the main purposes of the Athor Soul Exchange was to afford the Council of Sirius an opportunity to monitor the experiences of Athor in order to understand the tremendous negativity experienced here on Earth. Prior to this, these Beings of Light were totally out of touch with what we

Earthlings perceive as reality, since they had never incarnated on Earth. This situation is similar to what I often observed in the university system when a college professor was attempting to instruct ~~~~ teaching without having been in ~ ~

From ~~~

~~~ another aspect of the Athor ~~~ the very early history of this planet. This entity ~~ mythological Egyptian goddess Hathor. (I discovered that Athor and Hathor, in fact, are names used interchangeably for this well-known goddess.) Hathor, however, seems to have been an Extraterrestrial here on Earth directly from Sirius. Therefore, this was not an incarnation per se— that is, a birth through an Earth mother. She only materialized in a physical form when she wished to be seen, and this form was sometimes different depending on the situation.

There are numerous references to Hathor in *The Sirius Mystery*, a book by Robert Temple, which presents the theory that extraterrestrials from Sirius had visited Earth many thousands of years ago. "Hathor seems to be meant to represent the actual Sirius system, the 'house' or area in the celestial regions" (p. 169).

Athor has been extremely resistant to exploring this connection with Hathor. She is strongly opposed to any elitist philosophy where one soul is considered superior to another. She constantly has insisted that "We Are One" and that all souls will evolve at their own pace. No one is better than anyone else. She has no desire to be considered a goddess.

The Rose soul contributed to the experiment by allowing her brain to be rewired and a probe implanted by the extraterrestrials when she was the professor in the Himalayas in her most recent lifetime. The Rose soul triggered the allergies by dying a most agonizing death in a past life from eating a poisonous fungus plant. She further contributed to the experiment through suffocation by molds in the hay in another lifetime, leading to one of the chief reasons that the Rose body has Environmental Illness in this lifetime.

Since the Rose soul first differentiated as a separate consciousness on Alpha Centauri, it seems most appropriate that a being from Alpha Centauri entered the auric space of the professor in the Himalayas to prevent the body from dying. Perhaps (and this is only theoretical) there had been some previous connection on Alpha Centauri between this extraterrestrial being and the Rose soul when it resided there.

At any rate, the work on the brain of the professor was preparation for the brain to be highly psychic in Rose during this lifetime. There are indications of this prior to the actual exchange because the child Rose was very much attuned to the ET "visitors" she considered her real parents when she was still in the crib. This ET experiment resulted, however, in spiritual shock for the professor, and this was carried over into the auric vehicles of the Rose soul in this lifetime. The result of the damage to the auric vehicles contributed greatly to the Rose-Athor body being open to absorbing the negativity of all she encountered.

Most of this discussion thus far has dealt with the karmic reasons for which Athor made the Soul Exchange. Now we need to determine what her particular service to Earth is supposed to be, keeping in mind that Athor is only one of these highly evolved beings now in Earth bodies. From my perspective, I believe that this therapy process was extremely important in order to inform other therapists and the scientific community that a Soul Exchange is a valid phenomenon. These "New Beings" are some of our most advanced teachers, and they need to be able to come "out of the closet" at this point in our evolution.

Athor would not have sought therapy from me had she not been afflicted with Environmental Illness. Further, the Athor readings are revealing other types of experiments, which will be written about in future books and which also need recognition, particularly by therapists, because all of these experiments are puzzling and traumatic when there appears to be a total change in personality, although the experiment may not be an actual Soul Exchange.

These "New Beings" are vital to the evolution of people on Earth into a new species, which is happening even now, whether we are aware of it at a conscious level or not. These are my own understandings of this particular Soul Exchange experiment. From a cosmic perspective, it has been a grand and glorious experiment. Perhaps parts of the scheme did not work out as planned but, overall, I find the "plot" totally ingenious, and I expect to gather even more fascinating data about other souls and their "cosmic plan" as we continue the Athor Soul Readings.

"*Regarding the experience in the womb of the being from Alpha Centauri: there is this huge blob that just engulfs everything. It's disgusting.... I'm going inside the blob...turning, turning, turning, round and round and round. There is this sucking motion and a vortex of energy that is most crude. It just spins everything and sucks everything and engulfs everything, and I feel trapped. I feel trapped! (Whispering) I see an image of this tiny human figure inside this round ovum, and it's just turning and turning inside. I feel trapped. I feel trapped like I did in the cave in this strange body which was not human and I don't know what it was. The ears were angular and came to a point. And the head was very different from the human head. The skin was of a much thicker quality and had a different coloration to it, almost like a greenish, grayish, brownish color. It did not have a human appearance. This is a very difficult memory to resurrect from the cellular memory ...*"

— *Athor, July 16, 1989*

Chapter 18

Epilogue

Evelyn

A side from Athor's continuous illness, there were further delays in completing this book. We had begun the final revision in late 1994 when my husband, Wally, was diagnosed with acute leukemia. He had been disabled for several years, but it came as quite a shock to discover that he had leukemia. His transition came within two months after the diagnosis.

After several blood transfusions, he developed pneumonia and was in the hospital for a week, then transferred to a skilled nursing facility in the hope that he could regain some strength through physical therapy. He was in a hospice program; thus, when there was no improvement, I made the decision to bring him home to make his transition.

After only a few days at home he lapsed into a coma and left his body in early October, 1994. Wally was totally supportive of our book, although he never read any of it, stating that he would not understand it. Strangely, even though his scientific mind could not accept the spiritual concepts presented through my work with Athor, Wally seemed to admire me sincerely for what I was doing and gave me strong encouragement to continue on my chosen path.

Athor assures me that although Wally is still being administered to in a spiritual "hospital" two months after his passing, he will soon be able to play for a while and do many of the things he was physically unable to do for many years. He loved the outdoors but was confined to the house for most of the past six years.

After that, he will go on to various schools of learning where, for the first time since he began his Earthly incarnations, he will be able to make the connection between his last Earth life and his existence in the spiritual dimensions.

Although it was a very difficult marriage at times, we had an extremely close soul bond and I felt that I had a soul contract to stay with Wally until his transition. Athor tells me that Wally's soul gained much spiritual growth through his exposure to my spiritual beliefs, even though this was not apparent on an Earth personality level.

Because of my work with many clients who are in similar relationships, I would like to offer encouragement to any mate who has volunteered at a soul level to help the other soul in its evolution. Although diff... for both people, such an agreement off... portunity f...

...way, I received some valuable information concerning the Council of Sirius. I had always wondered if anything else ever had been written about the Council of Sirius. When I voiced this query during a public lecture I was presenting in Sacramento, a member of the audience suggested that I read *The Rays and the Initiations*, one of the series of Alice Bailey books.

Taking this advice, I found many references to Sirius in the book, including the following statement: "These ancient Mysteries were originally given to humanity by the Hierarchy, and were—in their turn—received by the Hierarchy from the Great White Lodge on Sirius" (pp. 330-331). I asked Athor what the connection, if any, was between the Great White Lodge and her Council. She said that they were one and the same, explaining that the Council is one part of the Great White Brotherhood. She apparently thought I knew this, but we had never discussed it, nor did this information come through any of the therapy sessions. This bit of knowledge gave me increased validation that the Athor story is indeed true.

Throughout the three years I worked with Athor, I had continued to wonder just why I was involved in this kind of research. In October, 1991, I had a regression with Shirley-Am-Ork, another person who thought she was a Soul Exchange. Since Shirley is a hypnotherapist herself, I asked her to do a hypnosis session with me. During the session I stated that agreements for Soul Exchanges take place in another dimension. The souls interested in such an exchange meet with a council. If the council agrees that the exchange would be beneficial, various souls are "interviewed" to determine which souls would best be able to meet the needs of one another. After this is determined by the council, then the souls are granted permission to make the exchange at a particular projected time in the future. We have learned that there are many councils with various functions throughout the Universe. This, however, is not one of the functions of the Council of Sirius.

This was rather astounding information to me, since I had certainly never read about this anywhere. However, it did seem like a very logical and good plan. Since I do not consider myself a particularly good hypnotic subject (I have great difficulty with visualization), I was truly amazed when this information came through my own mind.

I finally asked Athor if she could validate this in early 1992. The following information came from Athor:

A: This being (Evelyn) was a member of the council, or a certain group of beings, which were involved with organization and workings of this type of Soul Exchange phenomenon. As a member of the Council, this being was responsible for helping to choose those from her realm and her sphere who were desirous of participating in such an exchange. There are many levels and many planes herein. These are exchanges which occur quite frequently, though they are not necessarily on what you would term a soul level, as Light beings and Light bodies often do exchange, but not in the manner in which you presently view it, for it is a different phenomenon when it occurs with soul bodies through the Earth sphere.

These particular beings exchanged other energies and frequencies more so than actual soul bodies, per se. It is a very fine distinction here because these realms and levels are not so dense and Light bodies are an easy matter to exchange between beings of similar density. It is not such a laborious project as it is when trying to bridge the gap between various densities wherein it is necessary for the Soul Exchange to occur, and there is more of a certain feeling of imprisonment due to the disparity in dimensional frequencies. It was like beings came in front of members of this group and said they would wish to learn this and experience that, and move to this plane and dimension, etcetera, and the beings on this council made recommendations and decisions based on these desires and needs, so this one, Evelyn, was in that capacity.

E: Could you tell me more about the council? How many members were on the council?

A: This particular one was composed of nine members. The council was more similar to an interplanetary or interdimensional system. It was between a dimension and a system, so it was not quite in—how would you say this? There are planetary systems out there which have physical basis in reality today, such as the sphere called the Sun, which is the physical representation of many energies. This place where you were on the council did not have a physical representation of its system.

Evelyn

I still have difficulty accepting the fact that I was on a council of Beings of Light, but I also wonder how I could possibly know about this other dimension where the agreements regarding Soul Exchanges take place. I doubt that I could make up such a story, and I certainly have never read this anywhere that I am aware of at a conscious level. At any rate, assuming that this is really true, it would explain a great deal about my almost obsessive need to talk and write about the Soul Exchange phenomenon.

In considering all the infor~~mation th~~

~~... ...... sense~~ at a deep level, and I can accept the "facts" as possible truth. However, I still have great difficulty accepting that the Athor soul was involved in forming the Spiritual Matrix of the creation of the Earth. Maybe part of my problem with this is seeing Athor in a human body with many human problems and trying to match this up with this very esoteric concept.

I have been reading many books over the past year dealing with creation of the Earth: books on the Kabbala, the *Earth Chronicles* by Zecharia Sitchin, books concerning Lemuria and Atlantis—any material I could find on the creation of the Earth. All tell the story from somewhat different perspectives. I have been trying to fit all of the information together and have yet to reach any totally satisfactory conclusions.

I offer the Athor concept as simply a possibility. Again, believe only what resonates as truth for you. We are living at a very exciting time in the evolution of the Earth. To survive our ever-changing reality, we all need to be open minded. Through my work with Athor, I can, however, state with certainty: we all come from the same Source: WE ARE ONE.

Athor

While we were working on the final draft, Evelyn felt that I should include a description of all of my kundalini experiences. Weaving them chronologically into my autobiography would have been impossible, as I now have difficulty remembering accurately in what years they occurred, so I am including them here. My first kundalini experience was described previously in my autobiography, so I will go on to the other experiences.

The second and third kundalini experiences occurred while I was attending a group meditation led by followers of a famous "guru" from India. A friend, Martha, and I went to San Francisco to participate in these group meditations. While I was moving and jumping to the beat of the taped music designed to raise one's kundalini, that strange feeling once again rose from the base of my spine.

Once more the kundalini erupted with such force that I was lifted physically off the ground and thrown from a horizontal position in mid-air into the wall backwards, head-first. I lay dazed, in a crumpled heap on the floor. After a few minutes of reorienting myself, I left the hall and lay down on a couch in another room for ten or fifteen minutes to rebalance my body and process this experience.

That evening, Martha and I joined a few other "devotees'" for dinner in a neighboring restaurant. During dinner, I felt the now familiar energy uncoiling at the base of my spine. I told Martha that the kundalini was about to rise again and we hurried back to the meditation center. By then, the energy had moved to my solar plexus, or third chakra area. I lay on the floor and became extremely nauseous as the energy churned and rotated repeatedly in my solar plexus. As the churning and spinning in that chakra continued, I became increasingly more fearful, as the room was spinning in relentless circles. Lying flat on the floor with the entire room spinning, I begged Martha to hold my feet tightly and not let go.

The spinning sensation was so severe that that I felt I would spin out of my body into oblivion if Martha did not ground me by holding my feet. The dizzying spinning lasted one hour and suddenly stopped, as abruptly as it had begun. We went to bed in our rooms and after a normal night's sleep, left the center for home the next morning.

Though I had cried out for help while lying on the floor that evening to any of the other one-hundred-some "devotees" who were also staying there, not one single person came to help. Whether they simply couldn't hear my anguished cries as I lay there with the room spinning relentlessly, or they didn't wish to respond, I don't know. I do know, however, that after that experience, Martha and I severed our connection with that movement.

The fourth and final kundalini experience occurred one to two years later. This experience was by far my most pleasant one. Again, as on the three previous occasions, the kundalini stirred and rose without warning. This time it rose in a balanced fashion up both sides of my spine, traveling an entwined, braided circuit to the top of my head. Instead of being locked at the top as in my first experience many (possibly fifteen) years ago, it exited through the top of my head in continuous showers of white Light. For four hours, I was bathed in a waterfall of luminescent white Light cascading out from the crown of my skull, spilling all around me in a most marvelous ecstasy of peace, love, joy, and life. Four hours later the Light abated, and I went to bed physically exhausted once more.

Those four kundalini experiences did not leave me with conclusions of "Eureka, I have found it!" Rather, I believe they were simply four experiences in a lifetime of occurrences that helped open certain energy centers and expanded my awareness much further. As a result of these continuous spiritual occurrences, I have been permitted access to numerous realms and dimensions in "My Father's Kingdom." It is with great reverence, awe, and gratitude that I thank the All That Is for this blessing.

I pray and fervently hope that more and more people will also experience the ecstasies of discovering an unbounded Universe. The joys of such discovery cannot be matched by anything else ~~~~~~

deepest ~~~~~~

~~~~~~ spheres. It is that music ~~~~~~ reverberates through each and every cell of each being. We delight in its frequencies and harmonies, for we truly have composed it and sung it for eons.

God Bless!

Glossary

All That Is: The Creator, God; the energy of which everything is made; the Sea of Life on all levels.

Adamic strain: The label given to the first stable prototypical model of homo sapiens.

Akashic records: A complete history of a soul's life cycles and existences from the original point of differentiation from the Source, the All That Is. Athor views these records as a sequence of events, as in viewing a movie.

Alpha Centauri: A triple star system that is the brightest celestial object in the constellation Centaurus.

Angelic Realm: That substratum of the Celestial Kingdom which has always maintained a certain vibrational level of singular frequencies. This realm is where angels are born and come from. It is a non-changing realm in the sense that the growth produced within it is not seen as human growth is seen. The frequencies have a purity to them. They are very selective. All the frequencies in the Angelic Realm come together in a cohesive, whole, singular frequency; thus, it is very different from the Earth plane.

Androgynous: A state where there is a balance between the masculine and feminine aspects of a being, and sometimes one where there is no sexuality, as in many Beings of Light who do not reproduce or have sexual expressions as humans do. "Asexual" is often used synonymously with "androgynous," though they do not have quite the same meaning.

Auric body/auric field: The life force energy surrounding human beings and animals which is scientifically measurable. The auric field contains the etheric, emotional, mental, and causal bodies. All these bodies assume a certain shape which conforms around the etheric vehicle, so they are often seen as layers, and yet as flashing lights and energies as well. For an individual who has achieved a full opening of inner sight, they are very multidimensional to view.

Causal vehicle: That level of frequency in which the soul seeds or samskaras of all beings lie. It is the repository of future learning.

Celestial Kingdom: The kingdom from which the devas, fairies, and angels originate.

Chakras: Energy vortexes that allow a being to both draw from the universal life force and life stream and to contribute to it as well. They could be compared to respiratory organs in their process of intake and outflow. This is the main function of the chakras; without them there would be no life.

D___'

... a location.

...s reality is expressed primarily in seven levels, though each level has sub-levels within it.The Earth is in third density, moving into fourth.

Devic: In Sanskrit, a Deva is a god or divinity; one of an order of good spirits. In western metaphysics, the devic energy is the spirit consciousness of mineral, plant, animal, and more subtle forms of fairies.

DNA: The abbreviation for deoxyribonucleic acid, which is a compound found in chromosomes and is a long chain molecule comprising many repeated and varied combinations of four nucleotides. Subdivisions of the molecules are believed to be genes. DNA is the major repository of genetic information.

Double helix: Shape found in the normal, two-stranded human DNA.

Emotional vehicle: Often called the astral vehicle, it links the higher subtle bodies such as the causal, mental, and emotional with the etheric and physical bodies. It is through the emotional vehicle that the higher energies are stepped down so that they can be utilized in and through the physical realm. Only in the physical realm is there a need for an emotional body; all other, non-physical realms do not have emotional bodies.

Environmental Illness: An immune system disruption that makes a person react to pollens, molds, chemicals, foods, and/or inhalants in a variety of maladaptive ways. Some of these reactions may include periodic or continuous digestive disturbances, severe pains anywhere in the body or head, respiratory distress, mental fatigue, inability to walk or stand, changes in heart rhythms, and a host of other symptoms.

Etheric: The holder of all unseen events. All things exist first as ideas or thought-forms in the etheric before manifestation into the physical.

Extraterrestrial: A being who is not of Earth, but from some other planet, star, or dimension.

Fourth Dimension: A dimension regarded by scientists as time, and considered along with the three spatial dimensions of height, width, and length. It is an etheric dimension that provides the pathway to the Higher Worlds.

Frequency: The rate at which molecules, energy, or consciousness vibrate; all matter is vibrating energy.

Higher Self: That part of one's self that links one's mind and body to higher truths and realities, allowing an expansion of awareness and truth to take place in one's consciousness.

Humanoid: A body having the qualities and attributes of *Homo Sapiens*.

Hypnosis session: A form of therapy wherein an altered state of mind and body is induced through relaxation in order to assist a client to recall and/or release traumatic experiences and memories.

Karma: The Hindu concept of the continuation of the soul after physical death and its repeated incarnations in different bodies at different time periods in order to balance out the lessons it incarnates to learn.

Kundalini: The primordial energy housed at the base of the spine which, when fully activated, rises up the spinal column through each chakra, culminating with the crown chakra at the top of the head. When kundalini has risen successfully by joining the negative and positive energies in a circuit up the spine, an individual may achieve cosmic consciousness or a fully enlightened state of consciousness. As it is such a powerful force, kundalini should be activated only under the guidance of one who has successfully raised his/her own kundalini fully, or who is sufficiently informed as to the benefits and dangers involved.

Left brain: The side of the brain that primarily controls logical, deductive reasoning and mathematical, scientific, and linear abilities.

Logoic Haven: A safe, secure place where one returns to rest, regenerate, and recuperate. The Logoic Haven is the haven of the Logos (the Central Sun). It is where all energies are transmuted. Simply put, it is an energy source.

Matrix: That which originates, develops, or encloses anything; a network of ideas that forms a symbiotic relationship; an archetypal template.

Medulla oblongata: The part of the brain located in the brain stem. This is an area which has a chakra located near it that is important in connecting and linking the triangular aspect of Light which is necessary in the head region.

Mental vehicle: The next frequency vibration beyond the astral or emotional vehicle, which is comprised, in the human case, of one's thoughts, thought currents, and thought energies.

Metaphysics: The branch of philosophy that deals with first principles and seeks to explain the nature of being or reality (ontology) and of the origin and structure of the world (cosmology). It is closely associated with the theory of knowledge, and with occult lore.

Necromancy: A form of magic or method of conjuration or divination through invocation of the dead.

Near Death Experience (NDE): A ~~~

~~~ which ~~~ leaving the physical body and going through a tunnel which opens into a bright white Light. Many people who have had NDEs report having seen loved ones at the end of the tunnel, or some new type of being. This being is then able to contribute to this planet on figure who may have a message for them. Others have seen colors and/or experienced a profound state of peace and pain-free bliss. NDEs may be part of the "New Being" experiments.

Plane: That substratum of energetic currents that constitutes the main subdivision of a dimension. There are many planes or subcurrents of energies within a dimension. They are, in a sense, like steps, but because the aspects of dimensions are not linear, this is not exactly correct terminology.

Poltergeist: In German, a mischievous ghost that bangs around and makes noises, turns lights on and off, and generally makes a nuisance of itself.

Possession: A negative activity, typically originating from karmic ties between two spirits, in which the "possessing spirit" takes over the body of the other. The other soul does not leave completely but is overshadowed by the possessing essence.

Reincarnation: Cycle of births and deaths in the physical and ethereal realms which is dictated by each individual soul's learning and lessons.

Seance: A gathering of individuals who are meeting specifically to attempt communication with the spirits of physically deceased individuals.

Soul Exchange Entity (S.E.E.): One who has experienced a Soul Exchange within this lifetime.

Shiva: The god of Hinduism who is the slayer of illusion.

Silver cord: An etheric band/cord of energy that connects the astral vehicle to the physical body through the third energy center (chakra) located at the solar plexus. This cord disconnects fully at the point of physical death.

Sirius: The Dog Star; the brightest appearing star in the heavens located in the constellation Canus Major. It lies 8.7 light years from Earth. According to information channeled through Sheldon Nidle, Sirius is a multi-star system composed of nine stars. (See *You Are Becoming A Galactic Human* in bibliography.)

Solar Logos: That aspect of the "All That Is" which is a form of evolution far beyond present human comprehension. There is nothing in it remotely resembling the human condition. All energies from the Solar Logos are filtered and transformed, rather than beamed directly onto this planet. There has to be a stepping-down mechanism, as the voltages of this energy are beyond human description.

Soul Braid: An interdimensional experiment in which one soul Light fuses with at least one other (and sometimes more) soul Light(s) to produce a more levels than it might have had it remained a singular soul. Some Soul Braids are effected because one soul essence never has been incarnated before and is so unfamiliar with the Earth plane that it could not successfully complete its cycle of service to the planet or to other beings by itself. If the fusion is ultimately successful, it produces a stronger, more adaptable being who is familiar with both this dimension and others, providing a link to these other dimensions and realities. It is another experiment that souls try in expressing the creative aspect of Divinity.

Soul Exchange: An experience wherein the soul Light vivifying a physical vehicle leaves and is replaced by another soul essence—often in a Near Death Experience though not necessarily limited to NDEs. An agreement between the incoming soul essence and the departing essence has been made long before, in prior lifetimes or between lifetimes, so this type of exchange is different from a case of spirit possession in which the agreement does not originate in a positive manner.

Soul Reading: A psychic reading in which the individual's soul history is viewed through accessing the Akashic records, which contain a complete history of that soul's lifetimes and existences from the original point of differentiation from the Source, the All That Is.

Third Eye: The psychic energy center corresponding to the pineal gland, or medulla plexus, between the eyebrows, called "Ajna chakra" in Hinduism. It is the seat of clairvoyance or the ability to see beyond the normal senses, and reveals the insight of the future.

UFO Contactee: An individual who has had some type of contact with Unidentified Flying Objects (UFOs), an extraterrestrial entity, or other unexplained phenomenon (not including ghosts, apparitions, etc.) which seems to have its origins off-Earth.

11:11: An event celebrated worldwide on January 11, 1992 to activate a pre-encoded cellular memory to open the doorway to a Higher Dimension.

Selected Bibliography

Amidon, Horton E. *Cross-Correspondence Among The Loehr-Daniels Life Readings.* Gnosticoeurs Publishers, Grand Island, FL. 1985.

Bailey, Alice. *The Rays And The Initiations.* Lucis Publishing Company, New York. 1960.

Bassett, Noble P. *Constitution Of The United Nations Of The World.* Christopher Publishing House, Boston, MA. 1944.

Cerve, Wisher. *Lemuria-The Lost Continent Of The Pacific.* A.M.O.R.C. Rosicrucian Park, CA. 1959.

Chaney, Earlyne. *Initiation In The Great Pyramid.* Astara, Inc., Upland, CA. 1987.

Churchward, Col. James. *The Children Of Mu.* BE Books. Albuquerque, NM. 1992.

Elkins, Don, Carla Rueckert and James Allen McCarty. *The Book Of One: The Ra Material.* LL Research, Louisville KY. 1984.

Essene, Virginia and Sheldon Nidle. *You Are Becoming A Galactic Human.* S.E.E. Publishing Company, Santa Clara, CA. 1994.

Halevi, Z'ev ben Shimon. *A Kabbalistic Universe.* Samuel Weiser, Inc., York Beach, ME. 1977.

Hope, Murry. *Ancient Egypt: The Sirius Connection.* Element Books, Great Britain. 1990.

Hussey, Helen and Sandra Sherrod. *Dr. John: He Can Read Your Past Lives.* Gnosticoeurs Publishers, Grand Island, FL. 1983.

Kieffer, Gene. *Kundalini For The New Age; Selected Writings Of The Gopi Krisna.* Bantam Books, New York. 1988.

Loehr, Franklin. *Diary After Death.* Religious Research Press, Grand Island, FL. 1986.

Loehr, Franklin. *Death With Understanding.* Religious Research Press, Grand Island, FL. 1987.

Loehr, Franklin. *The Development of Religion As A Science.* Gnosticoeurs Publishers, Grand Island, FL. 1983.

Milanovich, Dr. Norma. *We, The Arcturians.* Athena Publishing, Albuqueque, NM. 1990

Milanovich, Dr. Norma and **Dr. Shi-**
You F

...ens Among Us. Ballantine Books, New York. 1985.

Montgomery, Ruth. *Threshold to Tomorrow.* Ballantine Books, New York. 1982.

Montgomery, Ruth. *Strangers Among Us.* Ballantine Books, New York. 1979.

Montgomery, Ruth. *A World Beyond.* Ballantine Books, New York. 1971.

Papastavro, Tellis. *The Gnosis And The Law.* Group Avatar, PO Box 41505, Tuscon, AZ. 1972.

Parrish-Harra, Carol W. *Messengers of Hope.* New Age Press, Black Mountain, NC. 1983

Ring, Kenneth. *The Omega Project.* William Morrow and Company, New York. 1992.

Roberts, Helen. *Karma, The Great Teacher.* Gnosticoeurs Publishers, Grand Island, FL. 1985.

Robinson, Lytle. *Story Of The Origin And Destiny Of Man.* Berkeley Publishers Group, New York. 1976.

Royal, Lyssa and Keith Priest. *Prism Of Lyra.* Light Technology and Royal Priest Research Press. Scottsdale, AZ. 1989.

Sitchin, Zecharia. *The 12th Planet.* Avon Books, New York. 1976.

Sitchin, Zecharia. *The Stairway To Heaven.* Avon Books, New York. 1980.

Sitchin, Zecharia. *The Wars Of God And Men.* Avon Books, New York. 1985.

Sitchin, Zecharia. *The Lost Realms.* Avon Books, New York. 1990.

Snow, Chet, Ph.D. and **Helen Wambach, Ph.D.** *Mass Dreams of the Future.* McGraw-Hill, New York, NY. 1989

Spalding, Baird. *Life And Teachings Of The Masters Of The Far East; Volumes I, II, III, and V.* DeVorss and Co., Marina Del Rey, CA. 1955.

Stern, Jess. *Edgar Cayce The Sleeping Prophet.* Bantam Books, New York. 1968.

Stevenson, Ian, M.D. *Twenty Cases Suggestive Of Reincarnation.* University Press Of Virginia, Charlottesville, VA. 1974.

Stone, Julita M. *Researching The Soul On Two Realms.* Religious Research Press, Grand Island, FL. 1991.

Streiber, Whitley. *Communion.* William Morrow, New York. 1987.

Sugre, Thomas. *The Story Of Edgar Cayce: There Is A River.* A.R.E. Press, Virginia Beach, VA. 1945.

Temple, Robert. *The Sirius Mystery.* Destiny Books, Rochester, VT. 1976.

Wambach, Helen, Ph.D. *Reliving Past Lives.* Barnes & Noble, New York. 1984.

Weiss, Brian, M.D. *Through Time Into Healing.* Simon And Schuster, New York. 1992.

Wilkins, Juelle. *The WalkIn.* Bookpartners, Inc. Wilsonville, OR.1995

Williamson, George Hunt. *Other Tongues, Other Flesh.* Amherst Press, Amherst, WI. 1954.

Woodward, Mary Ann. *Edgar Cayce's Story Of Karma.* Berkeley Publishing Company, New York. 1971.

Zonatar, Kathryn. *Soul Exchange.* O.M.R.A., Sacramento, CA. 1991.

About the Authors

Evelyn Fuqua holds a B.A. in Psychology from Agnes Scott College
M.A. in Counseling from California
Ph.D.

~~~~~~ was
~~~~~~~~~~~~~~~~~~~~~~~~~~ counselor in the public schools. Dr. Fuqua
has presented many workshops at professional conferences. She served on the Board of Directors of the Association of Past Life Research and Therapies and as State Relations Chairman for the California State Counselors Association. She is the author of a manual and album on self esteem. Currently Dr. Fuqua is in private practice in Rocklin, California.

Rose-Athor is a Soul Exchange from the star system of Sirius who took on the body of the former occupant when it was three years, two months old. As a result of this exchange, she was afforded the opportunity to experience life in a body and to contribute to the "spiritual awakening" and grounding of Light frequencies occurring on Earth at this time. Athor is able to read the Akashic records and trace souls back to their soul origins and extraterrestrial existences. She has counseled individuals for approximately thirty years as her health permits. Athor resides in the Sierra Nevada foothills with her husband.

To contact Dr. Fuqua or to obtain more information about the Athor readings, send a SASE to:

Oakdell Multidimensional Research Association,
PO Box 2063,
Rocklin, CA 95677

Publisher's Comment

Our mission and purpose is to publish ascension books and complementary material for all peoples and all children worldwide. We urge you to share the information with your friends, and to join our network of spiritually-oriented people.

We currently serve over fifty authors, musicians, and artists. They need your support to get their messages to all nations. Our financial proceeds are recycled into producing new ascension books and expanding our distribution worldwide. If you have been financially blessed by the universe and would like to support this important endeavor, we ask you to consider becoming an investor in Oughten House. Please contact us.

Ascension

An Ascension Handbook, by Tony Stubbs. A practical presentation which describes the ascension process in detail and includes several exercises to help you integrate it into your daily life. With humor and warmth, it brings ascension to "where we live," treading lightly but firmly over such topics as love, power, and truth; energy and matter; breaking old patterns; aligning with Spirit; and life as a Lightworker.
— ISBN 1-880666-08-1, $12.95

What Is Lightbody? Archangel Ariel, channeled by Tashira Tachi-ren. Offers a twelve-level model for the ascension process, leading to the attainment of our Light Body. Recommended in *An Ascension Handbook*, this book gives many invocations, procedures, and potions to assist us on our journey home. Related tapes available.
— ISBN 1-880666-25-1, $12.95

Heart Initiation, by Julienne Everett. Speaks to the seeker on the path who wants to know how to become totally free and why love is so important to freedom, whether ascension has to be difficult and painful, or whether there is an easier way, and what are the challenges and rewards of conscious ascension.
— ISBN 1-880666-36-7, $14.95

My Ascension Journal by Nicole Christine. Transform yourself and your life by using the journalizing methods given in this book. Includes several real-life examples from the author's own journals, plus many blank pages on which to write your own ascension story. This quality bound edition will become a treasured keepsake to be re-read over and over again.
— ISBN 1-880666-18-9, $11.95

Cosmic Tales

The Corporate Mule: Don't Give Up Your Soul for the Company Goal, by Robert V. Gerard. In this "slice-of-life" novel, follow Scott, an idealistic ~~~~~~~~~~~~~~ corporate politics...and a very rude

his self-destructive ~~~~~~~~~~~~~~
— ISBN 1-880666-04-9, $14.95

Lady From Atlantis, by Robert V. Gerard. Shar Dae, the future empress of Atlantis, is suddenly transported onto a rain-soaked beach in modern America. There she meets her twin flame and discovers her mission: to warn the people of planet Earth to mend their ways before Mother Earth takes matters in her own hands!
— ISBN 1-880666-21-9, $12.95

Voice in the Mirror: Will The Final Apocalypse Be Averted? by Lee Shargel. In this first novel of The Chulosian Chronicles, Lee skilfully weaves fact and fiction to tell a thrilling story of extraterrestrials using the Hubble telescope to warn of impending planetary disaster. But that's only the beginning!
— ISBN 1-880666-54-5, $23.95 (Hardcover)

Cosmic Wisdom

The Extraterrestrial Vision by Gina Lake. Through Gina, Theodore, a nonphysical entity, tells us what we need to know about our extraterrestrial heritage and how to prepare for direct contact with those civilizations which will soon be appearing in our midst.
— ISBN 1-880666-19-7, $13.95

ET Contact: Blueprint for a New World by Gina Lake. Through Gina, the Confederation of Planets tells us what life on Earth will be like following mass contact with extraterrestrials, and what we must do to prepare in terms of changing institutions such as education, religion, politics, economics, the media, and most important, how we personally must change.
— ISBN 1-880666-62-6, $12.95

The Angels of the Rays by Johanna. A set of twelve lavish, full color Angel pictures with supporting descriptions and invocations. Includes 12 push-out full-color cards, one for each Angel. *Makes a stunning gift!*
— ISBN 1-880666-34-0, $19.95. (Additional card sets $12.95)

Self-Help & Transformational Tools

Intuition by Design, by Victor R. Beasley, Ph.D. A boxed set of 36 IQ (Intuition Quotient) Cards contain consciousness-changing geometry on one side and transformational verse on the other. The companion book tells you the many ways to use the cards in all aspects of your life. An incredible gift to yourself and someone you love. Highly recommended for bringing your life into alignment with the Higher Mind of Source.
— ISBN 1-880666-22-7, $21.95

Navigating the 90s by Deborah Soucek. Practical ways to deal with today's chaotic times, and claim your sovereignty when others would trample it. Focuses on ways of freeing ourselves from our past conditioning and imprinting, and provides simple, yet overlooked advice in reclaiming our true selves. Packed with pertinent observations and useful exercises.
— ISBN 1-880666-47-2, $13.95

Gifts: Remembering the Now, by Yolanda Zigarmi Martin. An ten-year-old girl, terrified of God ... a Crusader dying of battle wounds ... a distraught French noblewoman ... a shaman of the distant past—and future! In this true story, the author spontaneously relives her soul's other incarnations and learns from them, thus proving, once and for all, the continuity of the soul, the simultaneity of all incarnations, and that our incarnations interact with each other. A journey of transformation that truly pushes back the boundaries of awareness and takes you from your small self to the full glory of your True Self.
— ISBN 1-880666-59-6, $13.95

Design Your Intention: An Experience in Embodying Source, by Ruth Ford-Crenshaw. Join Ruth as she relives the "spiritual highs" of her path, and through her, meet such movers and shakers of the metaphysical world as Chris Griscom, Drunvalo, and Tashira Tachi-ren. Contains many invaluable excerpts from the spiritual classics.
— ISBN 1-880666-63-4, $12.95

Love and Hope: A Message for the New Millenium, by Kiyo Sasaki Monro. A delightfully written book of wisdom that the author has gleaned on her path, with autobiographical notes, and an extensive question-and-answer section derived from live presentations. An ideal "starter book" for someone new to metaphysics such as a gift for a friend.
— ISBN 1-880666-56-1, $14.95

Music Tapes and CDs

We carry m̶~̶

For a listing of availaoic unco,
card is bound into this book for your convenience, or you may reach us at
the location listed on the next page.

Attention: Businesses and Schools!

OUGHTEN HOUSE books are available at quantity discounts with bulk
purchases for educational, business, or sales promotional use. For details,
please contact the publisher.

Catalog Requests & Book Orders

Catalogs will gladly be sent upon request. Simply call the number below,
send in the Business R eply Card at the back of the book, or visit our on-
line Internet bookstore at the web site below.

Book orders must be prepaid: check, money order, international coupon,
VISA, MasterCard, Discover Card, and American Express accepted.

To place your order, call, fax, or mail to:

OUGHTEN HOUSE PUBLICATIONS
PO Box 2008
LIVERMORE · CALIFORNIA · 94551-2008 · USA
PHONE: (510) 447-2332
FAX: (510) 447-2376
E-MAIL: oughten@oughtenhouse.com
INTERNET: www.oughtenhouse.com